# SEA STORIES
# of DEVON

Introduced by
E.V. Thompson

BOSSINEY BOOKS

*First published in 1984
by Bossiney Books
St Teath, Bodmin, Cornwall
Designed, typeset and printed in Great Britain by
Penwell Ltd, Parkwood, Callington
Cornwall*



*© 1984 E.V. Thompson, Jim Butcher
Eric J. Grove, Michael Nix, Sandi Marshall
Sarah Foot, Monica Wyatt, Rosemary Anne Lauder
David Young*

*ISBN 0 906456 84 3*

# CONTENTS


**Introduction**
by E.V. Thompson . . . . . . . . . . . . . . . . . . . . . . . . . . . . . . . . . . . . . . . . . 4

**The Billy Ruffian**
by E.V. Thompson . . . . . . . . . . . . . . . . . . . . . . . . . . . . . . . . . . . . . . . . . 15

**Lifeboat in the Sky**
by Jim Butcher . . . . . . . . . . . . . . . . . . . . . . . . . . . . . . . . . . . . . . . . . . . 25

**The Royal Naval College, Dartmouth**
by Eric J. Grove . . . . . . . . . . . . . . . . . . . . . . . . . . . . . . . . . . . . . . . . . . 34

**The 'Sjofna' Service**
by Michael Nix . . . . . . . . . . . . . . . . . . . . . . . . . . . . . . . . . . . . . . . . . . . 49

**Holland 1**
by Sandi Marshall . . . . . . . . . . . . . . . . . . . . . . . . . . . . . . . . . . . . . . . . . 58

**Sir Francis Drake**
by Sarah Foot . . . . . . . . . . . . . . . . . . . . . . . . . . . . . . . . . . . . . . . . . . . . 68

**The Torbay Lifeboat**
by Monica Wyatt . . . . . . . . . . . . . . . . . . . . . . . . . . . . . . . . . . . . . . . . . . 78

**The King of Bucks**
by Rosemary Anne Lauder . . . . . . . . . . . . . . . . . . . . . . . . . . . . . . . . . . . 89

**Prince of Rogues—Lundy and Thomas Benson**
by David Young . . . . . . . . . . . . . . . . . . . . . . . . . . . . . . . . . . . . . . . . . . . 97

# INTRODUCTION
## by E.V. Thompson

Devon is a county of marked contrasts. Renowned for its equitable climate and rich, rolling farmland, it also encompasses the beautiful, mysterious, yet bleak, upland expanse of Dartmoor. Farther north, another moor spills over from Somerset into the county. Equally individualistic, Exmoor is an area of deep, hidden valleys and dark legend. It was here that Richard Doddridge Blackmore set his nineteenth-century classic novel, *Lorna Doone.*

Even more contrasting than the countryside, are Devon's coasts —and the county has *two,* each differing greatly from the other.

Devon's south coast, washed by the narrowing waters of the English Channel, is a skein of sheltered inlets and wooded estuaries reaching deep into the land, somewhat reminiscent of the fjords of Norway. This is a coastline beloved by generations of yachtsmen. After years of searching, many of them finally discover their perfect anchorage along this stretch of the Devon coast.

There are an abundance of beaches hereabouts, ranging from 'pocket handkerchief' sized sandy coves, to the three-mile expanse of Slapton Sands. This is the county of the 'English Riviera', with a wealth of popular seaside towns, and all that goes with them.

In the extreme south west of the county is Plymouth, one of the busiest and best-known of Great Britain's naval ports. Proud of its long naval tradition, Plymouth is steeped in centuries of seafaring history.

Along its northern coast, Devon feels the full weight of the mighty Atlantic, before the force of this great ocean is tamed by the confines of the Bristol Channel.

**'Along its northern coast, Devon feels the full weight of the mighty Atlantic . . .'** ▶

'Proud of its long naval tradition, Plymouth is steeped in centuries of seafaring history.' Here, on 4 December 1978 HMS *Ark Royal* comes home to Plymouth—for the last time.

This is a majestic, at times *awesome* coastline, dominated by lofty cliffs. For many centuries the sea reigned unchallenged here. The high cliffs, rearing like giant tombstones from the sea, guard the bones of countless mariners whose names would fill every square foot of the sea-lashed rocky faces.

To the east of this Devon coast the line of cliffs is occasionally broken, albeit reluctantly, it seems, to provide minute refuges for the smaller vessels that run before the fury of a westerly storm.

Heading westwards along this northern coastline, nature relents and provides Devon with some of its finest beaches, together with harbour facilities for boats of all sizes. The traditional boat-building yard of Appledore is here. So too is Bideford, a riverside town with quays adjoining the main road. This was the third most important port in the British Isles when Queen Elizabeth I was on the throne of England.

Queen Elizabeth was justly proud of her seamen. They had no equal in the world—and one in every six was a Devon man. The most famous of them all was Francis Drake, knighted by the Queen for his incredible exploits. The first Englishman to circumnavigate the world, Drake began and ended his journey in Plymouth Sound, where the island that now bears his name is a familiar and romantic sight. In *Sea Stories of Devon,* the reader can learn both fact and legend of this great man. His love of country was so great that it is claimed he has reached out from a watery grave to aid England at times of great national peril—just as he promised he would.

The sea has always brought out all that is best in man, but it has also unlocked the door to his baser nature. *Sea Stories of Devon* introduces us to both these traits and gives a fascinating insight into the part the sea has played in the lives of men and women of Devon.

For the writer, the sea is a never-ending source of stories. It is also a bountiful provider, and an inviting highway to the world—but it is an uncertain friend, merciless when confronted by fools, or those who treat it with contempt.

None are more aware of this than the fishermen of Devon, men

**'Devon's south coast is washed by the narrowing waters of the English Channel.' Below: Mothecombe. Right: The Parson and Clerk near Teignmouth.**

who are familiar with the ocean's many moods. For 160 years fishermen have formed the nucleus of lifeboat crews, those gallant men
who put to sea in appalling conditions to aid their fellow men.
Frequently risking death, they successfully challenge the right of
the sea to its annual sacrifice.

It is not surprising that so many pages of *Sea Stories of Devon*
are devoted to the exploits of the lifeboatmen. Their very name has
become synonymous with gallantry, courage and self-sacrifice.
Around the coasts of Devon, these admirable qualities have sometimes been strained to breaking-point. Since its inception, the
lifeboat service has saved the lives of almost 100,000 sailors, but the
men who man the lifeboats have paid a high price for their gallantry.

Some of the rescues included in this book are little known. Others,
such as the incredible feat performed by the Lynmouth lifeboatmen
in the final year of the nineteenth century have taken their rightful
place in the folklore of Devon's sea stories.

Not all these rescues have taken place beneath the towering cliffs

**'Bideford, a riverside town with quays . . .'**

of the north coast. Many men have been snatched from the sea in the busy shipping-lanes of the English Channel. One such rescue is described in these pages and the high degree of courage involved was recognised by the award of a gold medal to the coxswain of the lifeboat, and bronze medals to each of his crewmen.

There is a romance about offshore islands that defies analysis. Perhaps it is inherited from our ancestors, to whom even the shortest sea voyage was a frightening and uncertain adventure. In *Sea Stories of Devon* is told the remarkable story of Lundy, a granite island rising from the sea some twelve miles off the north coast of Devon. Steeped in historical legend, many men—even in recent times—have dreamed of ruling an 'independent' Lundy, untrammelled by the laws of the mainland. Few have achieved the success of Thomas Benson, referred to here as the 'Prince of Rogues'. His is an almost unbelievable tale of greed and disregard for authority.

On the mainland not many miles away from Lundy, is a small

**Branscombe: '. . . an abundance of beaches . . .'**

village where every household once bore the Braund family name. James Braund, the nineteenth-century family head, was a fisherman and pilot whose proud boast it was that in 40 years he had lost neither a vessel nor a life on the treacherous Bideford bar.

Inevitably in any collection of sea stories, the leading part in so many of the tales is taken neither by a personality, nor a place—but a ship. So it is here. In 'The Billy Ruffian', the story of HMS *Bellerophon's* long association with Plymouth is traced from the days when she was one of the proudest ships in Lord Nelson's fleet, to the ignominy of her final role. Largely unrecognised at her anchorage in the waters of the Hamoaze, she was rocked by the wake of a new generation of warships, none of whom would ever achieve her former glory.

Today, 150 years later, these same Plymouth waters are plied by a new class of warship, undreamed of by the sailors of Nelson's fleet. Powered by nuclear-fuelled engines and equipped with weapons capable of wiping out a whole fleet, great cigar-shaped vessels travel silently *beneath* the oceans of the world, sometimes never seeing the faraway lands whose coasts they patrol—some of them lands discovered by men who set forth from this same port, centuries before.

There would seem to be little to connect those sailors of old with this modern, nuclear-powered, underwater navy. Yet, in November, 1982, the link between the ancient and modern navies saw the light of day for the first time in seventy years, in the dry dock of Devonport's naval dockyard. Known as *Holland 1,* this diminutive submersible craft first proved at the turn of the century, that an underwater warship was a feasible vessel, and so became the forerunner of the modern submarine.

The story of its remarkable recovery from the seabed in the shadow of the Eddystone lighthouse, is told in *Holland I.* It is a fascinating and important inclusion in *Sea Stories of Devon.*

As I have already mentioned, the county of Devon, perhaps more than any other county in the British Isles, has been responsible for supplying first-class seamen for the country's navy for as long as Great Britain has had ships at sea. It is, therefore, highly appropriate that when it was decided to give young, newly-appointed naval officers tuition in their chosen calling, Devon should be selected as the site for this 'Naval Academy'.

For more than 120 years the Royal Naval College at Dartmouth

**It was appropriate that Dartmouth should
be chosen as the site for the Royal Naval College.**

has supplied officers for the navies of Great Britain and the Commonwealth countries. During this time, Dartmouth-trained officers have decided naval strategy and fought in every sea-battle in which ships of the Royal Navy have been engaged. During these years, battles have changed. Indeed, the whole concept of warfare has developed from tactics designed to bring a line of wooden-walled, sail-powered men-of-war into action, to the management of a modern navy going to war with guided missiles, air support, and all the fearful capabilities of a nuclear age.

To cope with these wide-ranging changes, Dartmouth Royal Naval College has had to progress *ahead* of the times. That it has been able to do so successfully is a credit both to the Royal Naval College, and to the service for which it was established.

The history of the Royal Naval College, Dartmouth, is related in *Sea Stories of Devon.*

In a way, this story is a microcosm of the book itself. It is the story of men who go from the shores of Devon to make their mark on the world. Men whose lives are inextricably bound to the sea and know all its many moods. Men who love the sea—yet know it well enough to fear it too.

Men whose exploits go to make up the SEA STORIES OF DEVON.

E.V. Thompson

# THE BILLY RUFFIAN

*E.V. THOMPSON is one of the most famous novelists living and working in the Westcountry. He has achieved huge national and international success with novels like* Chase the Wind *and* Ben Retallick. *He served in the Royal Navy, and his latest novel is* The Restless Sea. *His earlier Bossiney titles are* Discovering Bodmin Moor *and* Discovering Cornwall's South Coast.

There was an almost holiday atmosphere in Plymouth on Wednesday, 26 July 1815. Crowds manned every vantage point from Rame Head to Wembury Point, and all eyes were looking out to sea. At 10 a.m. a topsail was sighted on the horizon and the excitement increased as more people came from their homes and places of work to join the watchers.

Yet the waiting was not over, even now. It was a fine day with little breeze and, as befitted a great lady, the stately warship took her time, knowing that all England awaited her arrival. Not until four o'clock in the afternoon did the Royal Navy forecastle party on board the man-of-war knock out the pin that secured the anchor chain. Anchor and chain clattered into the waters of the Sound and the last sail was furled. HMS *Bellerophon* had arrived.

Immediately, every available boat in the port of Plymouth put out into the Sound, most of them hired at a grossly exorbitant fee to any man or woman whose curiosity was matched by an ability to pay. Latecomers were disappointed. They had to make do with a glimpse of the great ship through a telescope, many of which were provided on brief loan by enterprising, shorebound sailors.

At first, the watchers on shore saw as little as did those who had taken to the waters of the Sound so hurriedly. Within minutes of her

arrival the warship was surrounded by guard boats. Ordered to the scene by the government of Lord Liverpool, they efficiently kept the armada of small boats at bay. The curious would-be observers were forced to nurse their disappointment from a distance.

Not until 6 p.m. that day were the waiting crowds rewarded for their patience. Heralded by an unmistakable stir on the crowded upper deck of *Bellerophon,* a small and slightly corpulent figure with deceptively broad shoulders put in an appearance. Dressed in the green greatcoat of a Colonel of Chasseurs of the Guard, decorated with red cuffs and collar, gold epaulettes and with a star-shaped award on his chest, he barely acknowledged the salutes of the sailors and accepted the doffed caps of his fellows as no more than his due.

The man was Napoleon Bonaparte, late-Emperor of France, and regarded as the most brilliant general the world had ever known. Now, after surrendering to Captain Maitland on board HMS *Bellerophon,* Napoleon was a prisoner, an exile from his country. His army, once seemingly invincible, had received a shattering defeat at the hands of the Duke of Wellington on the hillside of Mont St Jean, known to the world as the site of the Battle of Waterloo.

It had been a bloody and hard-fought contest. The Duke of Wellington entered the battle with more than 60,000 troops. When it ended, one in four was a casualty. The French, who had begun the battle with a slight superiority of numbers, suffered much heavier losses.

The man standing on the deck of the British warship, gazing out over Plymouth Sound with a haughty disdain, bore the full responsibility for these appalling casualties. His arrogance was captured by a Plymouth artist, Charles Eastlake. The prints he produced, showing the deposed Emperor on board *Bellerophon* in Plymouth Sound, would one day adorn the walls of thousands of homes in Victorian Britain.

While *Bellerophon* was in Plymouth Sound, notice was given to Napoleon Bonaparte that he was to be exiled to the lonely island of St Helena, far out in the South Atlantic. He did not take the news well, threatening to commit suicide rather than submit to such a

**◀ The man on the deck of the British warship gazing out over Plymouth Sound was Napoleon Bonaparte.**

humiliating fate. One of his companions, the fiery Madame Bertrand, went farther. She actually climbed the mizzen chains with the intent of throwing herself overboard to drown in the waters of the Sound, but was pulled back by one of the ship's officers.

Although Napoleon had been responsible for the deaths of countless thousands of British soldiers and sailors, he had many admirers on shore. Word reached the government that some of these were planning to apply for a writ of *Habeas Corpus*—a legal move aimed at bringing Napoleon before a judge in a British court of law, in order that the legality of his detention and proposed exile could be brought into question. Immediately, *Bellerophon* was given orders to sail from Plymouth.

The great ship weighed anchor at 1 p.m. on Friday, 4 August 1805, to rendezvous with the abrasive Admiral Sir George Cockburn, whose ship, *Northumberland*, was to carry Napoleon Bonaparte and his entourage to the island exile.

A few sightseers, out in their boats to watch *Bellerophon* get underway, were rewarded with the sight of the dramatic Madame Bertrand acting out another of her 'suicide' attempts. Throwing open a window of Bonaparte's spacious cabin at the stern of the ship, she made a noisy, but not *too* determined bid to throw herself into the sea and was pulled back by members of Napoleon's staff.

The surrender of Napoleon Bonaparte on her decks was the last of a long series of historic events in which *Bellerophon* had been a participant. A 74-gun ship-of-the-line, she had been launched in 1786, at a cost to their Lordships of the Admiralty of £30,232 14s 3d. Designed by Sir Thomas Slade, who also designed *Victory*, the famous ship on which Nelson died at Trafalgar, *Bellerophon* was 138 feet long from end to end of her stout keel. Two thousand oak trees, each at least 100 years old, were used in her construction.

*Bellerophon* was destined to share many battle honours with her more famous sister ship. On 1 June 1794—the date known to naval historians as 'the glorious first of June'—*Victory* and *Bellerophon* fought under the command of Admiral Lord Howe, when he scored a notable victory over the French, off Ushant.

On 1 August 1798, *Bellerophon*—known affectionately to her crew as the 'Billy Ruffian'—was with Nelson's fleet at the fierce Battle of the Nile. By the time victory had been secured for the British fleet, *Bellerophon* had been dismasted and a third of her crew were either dead, or disabled.

It seemed that the 'Billy Ruffian' was destined to be where the noise of battle was loudest. At the Battle of Trafalgar, in 1805, perhaps the most famous sea battle of all time, *Bellerophon* was there with Admiral Nelson and his flagship, *Victory*. As the British fleet prepared for action, the ship's First Lieutenant piped the crew to dinner, stating that Englishmen fought better with a comfortable meal in their bellies. Minutes later *Bellerophon* plunged into battle, to become a part of the legend that still surrounds the memory of the brilliant Admiral Lord Nelson.

By the time the long battle drew to a close, the mighty *Bellerophon* was once more dismasted and her decks a tangle of splintered wood. Her captain was dead, so too were many of her gallant crew. In fact, *Bellerophon* ended the battle with 150 casualties, more than was sustained by any other ship in Nelson's fleet.

**It was here on the Hoe that the crowds waited
for the first sight of *Bellerophon* and Napoleon.**

On 5 December 1805, *Bellerophon* arrived in Plymouth Sound. To quote a newspaper report of the day, she 'looked like a great hulk, with three sticks stuck up for jury masts'.

The newspaper description was to prove prophetic, but not for a few more years.

*Bellerophon* was refitted after Trafalgar and performed sterling service during the Napoleonic wars. However, when Napoleon was transferred to *Northumberland* in 1815, her days as a proud ship-of-the-line had come to an end.

But Plymouth had not seen the last of the old 'Billy Ruffian'. In June 1826, a familiar, yet strangely subdued shape was towed into Plymouth Sound and moored off the dockyard's South Jetty. The yellow and black paint had gone. So too had her tall masts. To curious onlookers, the iron bars at her gunports gave a clue to her new role. Her new name left no room for doubt. *Bellerophon* was now the *Captivity*. She was a prison hulk.

Fitted out at Sheerness to accommodate 600 prisoners, *Captivity* would remain at the Devon port for ten years, well known to those who plied the waters of the Hamoaze.

During her earliest weeks, *Captivity* carried only a comfortable 80 prisoners, but this increased very quickly as men sentenced in the courts of the land shuffled on board in linked pairs, secured with heavy chains about ankles and wrists. *Captivity* was one of ten hulks anchored in English ports and they held almost 4,500 prisoners between them.

Prison hulks had been utilised for many years. Their original use had been to hold prisoners-of-war captured during America's war of independence, but for many years now they had taken criminals sentenced to transportation by the Assize Courts and Quarter Sessions.

Transportation sentences varied from seven years—to a lifetime. Those banished from England for long periods were deemed to be the fortunate ones by convicts who had sampled life on board these 'Criminal Academies'. Long-term transportation meant remaining on board the evil-smelling hulks only until a transport ship was available to convey them to the convict settlements of Australia. Others, serving shorter sentences, would remain on board the hulk.

Among the first to sample life on board *Captivity* were two young Devon men. John Deane, aged only seventeen, and Henry Jerrow, aged twenty, were found guilty of stealing a cheap watch from a simple old man, in Exeter. They stopped him in the street to ask the time. When he brought out his watch, they snatched it from him and ran off, only to be quickly caught and brought before the court. Both were given sentences of seven years transportation, the Exeter Recorder informing them that they were both very fortunate men. Had the slightest degree of violence been used against the old man, they would have been sentenced to death.

Once on board *Captivity*, both men would have been allotted a sleeping space measuring six feet by twenty inches. Here they would sling their hammocks when the hatches were battened down at 'lights out'. As they rubbed at chafed wrists and ankles, established prisoners would have told them what to expect on board their new 'home'.

For six days every week their day would begin at 5.30 a.m. Fifteen minutes later they would muster on deck to eat their breakfast and wash the decks. At 6.45 a.m. the prisoners would stow their hammocks on the deck and proceed ashore in irons to begin a day's work.

They were employed mainly in the construction of new dockyard buildings, many using granite from the quarries owned by the Treffry family, who occupied the great house of Place, in Fowey, a few miles along the Cornish coast. Other tasks performed by the convicts were repairing roads; unloading and loading vessels; painting ships; cleaning cables; and preparing lead shot for the ships of His Majesty King George IV's navy.

At twelve noon the prisoners returned to *Captivity* for their main meal of the day, but by 1.20 p.m. they were at work again, being kept hard at it until 5.45 p.m.

Back on board, each man was thoroughly searched and had his irons examined. Some nights, school classes were organised for those it was felt might reap benefit from the rudiments of education. On Saturday evenings, all prisoners were made to shave, in preparation for the Sunday parade, known as 'Divisions', which was followed by a church service.

Every evening, the prisoners were locked up and lights extinguished by nine o'clock. It was now, during these dark hours, that many prisoners were made to pay the full price for whatever crimes they had committed, at the hands of men who were the very dregs of human society. Among their number were convicts who had seen every facet of death, degradation and vice. Men to whom violence was a natural way of life. Some were palpably insane.

Into this world were thrown young men like the two convicted of theft at Exeter and others, like fifteen-year-old Issacher Binney who stole two pounds of candles from the changing room of Poldice mine, in Cornwall. Because he had been convicted of a similar offence before, his sentence was that he should be transported for fourteen years.

There were many others who came from backgrounds far removed from the conditions in which they were now forced to live. Leaders of the newly-emerging Trades Unions; political agitators; forgers. All were thrown into the hulks to live, or die, in the brutal world where even the gaolers dared not tread once the hatches had been battened down for the night.

Many failed to survive the harsh conditions that prevailed on board the prison ships. One survey revealed that as many as one in three prisoners died on board the hulks.

Some men were driven to suicide. Others tried to escape. A few, very few, were successful. Others were not. At the Somerset Lent Assize in 1827, Daniel Moore was sentenced to death for being at large before the expiration of his seven year term of transportation. Those who were caught attempting to escape were committed to the 'casket'. This was a hole, usually in the deep, dark depths of the ship, where they were left lying almost naked on a bed of straw, sometimes for weeks at a time.

Yet there were still those who remembered the great ship that *Captivity* had once been: when, as *Bellerophon,* she proudly flew the ensign of Great Britain on the high seas, ready to go into action in defence of freedom. In 1827, two pieces of oak were ordered to be cut from the ship and snuff-boxes were made from them to be presented to the crowned heads of Europe.

Towards the end of her time at Plymouth, *Captivity* was taking far fewer prisoners on board. Probably one of the last was the unfortunate William Bonathan, convicted at Exeter Assizes, in 1833. The sixty-nine year old Bonathan was indicted for forging a bill of exchange—the forerunner of our modern cheque—to the value of £15.

Bonathan had been in the habit of making out bills for a local butcher who was unable to read or write. One day the butcher came to him and said a certain Mr Furnneaux had given him a bill of exchange for fifteen pounds, but had forgotten to sign his name.

The butcher claimed that Furnneaux had authorised him to sign in his place and to present the bill of exchange. As the butcher was unable to write, he pointed out the place where the name was to be signed and asked Bonathan to sign Furnneaux's name for him. This Bonathan did, without knowing he was doing wrong, and deriving no advantage from the transaction. All the facts were admitted in court by the butcher and Bonathan was given many splendid references, including one from Mr Furnneaux himself. Despite this, Bonathan was found guilty of forgery and duly sentenced to be transported for life.

There was little room for mercy in the court rooms of the nineteenth century.

**The best of *Bellerophon's* aged English oak was made into panelling at Place in Fowey.**

Finally, in January 1836, after performing fifty years' service for her country, the varied career of HMS *Bellerophon* came to an end and she was sold by the Admiralty for the sum of £4,030.

Although the career of a great ship had come to an end, part of her was to live on, here in the Westcountry, not very many miles from the sea port of Plymouth, that had witnessed both her glory, and the degradation that accompanied her change of name.

The buyer of *Bellerophon* was a Treffry, of Place, the great house that is at the very heart of the Cornish port of Fowey. Brought to Fowey in 1836, *Bellerophon* was put in the hands of local ship-breakers. The bulk of her timbers would be used in the many mines in which Treffry had an interest, but the best of her aged English oak was made into panelling, to adorn the rooms of this wonderful old house.

It could hardly have been more appropriate. Just as *Bellerophon* had fought and won against the French, so too had Elizabeth Treffry, many years before. In 1497, this brave woman defended Place against French raiders who landed in strength and sacked the town about the house.

The figurehead of *Bellerophon*, together with many of her stern ornaments, are on view in the *Victory* Museum at Portsmouth. No doubt many of the stout oak timbers still survive too, hidden in the water-logged tunnels of long-forgotten Cornish mines.

The beautiful oak panelling remains, fittingly, in the Westcountry —within easy sailing distance of the port of Plymouth, the town that bore witness to the triumphs and the despair of the 'Billy Ruffian'.

# LIFEBOAT IN THE SKY

*JIM BUTCHER returned in 1949 to Barnstaple, where he was born, as editorial representative of the Western Morning News. He became a farmer 25 years ago and travelled to several European countries as the paper's agricultural correspondent. He was the first journalist to reach flood-battered Lynmouth after the 1952 disaster. He is now retired but is still busy at his typrewriter.*

This is the age of ultra-sophisticated ship-to-shore communication, radio beacons, helicopters and radar. It is very doubtful whether the plight of the fully-rigged three-master, the *Forest Hall*, would nowadays generate more than a professional response from the South West's rescue co-ordination network, followed perhaps by a couple of paragraphs in the regional press and a short TV and radio news item.

But on the night of 12 January 1899 things were far different. All that the watchers on shore knew was that an unknown ship was in trouble in the worst gale for years. The tide was flowing up the Bristol Channel. Experienced men calculated that whatever she was the vessel would soon be driven ashore by the gale. They had seen her distress rockets and in a treacherous seaway like the Bristol Channel that was all they needed to know.

On board the 1,900-ton *Forest Hall* matters had not reached the desperate stage. The master, Captain Scott, had managed to get two anchors down. True, his ship was dragging a little, but once aground on the cruel and rocky Exmoor coastline there would be precious little hope of the crew surviving.

Trouble had started when the towline between the *Forest Hall* and the Liverpool tug *Joliffe* had parted in the storm. But the tugmaster knew all about it and was well aware of the danger. He could see that the *Forest Hall* had got her anchors out and he must have decided to stand off for a while so that he could plan how, in these conditions, he could make fast another towline.

It was getting dark on this winter's afternoon and Captain Scott prudently decided that with a night of unknown dangers before him the time had come to fire distress signals. Observers along the coast saw the red flares amid the mist and murk of this terrible storm. But no-one knew her exact predicament or that there was a crew of thirteen men and five apprentices aboard.

One thing soon became obvious. It was impossible to launch the Watchet lifeboat. At least two people took immediate action. The Chief Officer of the Minehead Coastguards sent a telegram to the secretary of the Lynmouth lifeboat, fifteen miles down the coast, asking for help. Almost simultaneously a certain Mr Goddard, landlord of the Anchor Hotel, Porlock, despatched a similar message.

Mr E.J. Pedder, Lloyds agent at Lynmouth and signalman to the lifeboat, received both telegrams at around 7.52 p.m. Both messages put the *Forest Hall* at a few miles offshore and drifting helplessly towards certain disaster as the tide began to ebb. Even to this day mistakes occur in rescue bids. But on this night of all nights in January 1899 with the wind howling up-channel and mountainous seas breaking on the shore, it was not surprising that at least two people slightly misread the situation.

The *Forest Hall* was not helplessly adrift. Assistance was at hand in the shape of the tug *Jollife*. But to the Lynmouth lifeboat crew the picture was far different. Men were in serious danger of losing their lives. And as they battled with the gale blowing spray and spindrift horizontally across Lynmouth seafront, they knew it would be impossible to launch the Lynmouth boat on a night like this.

They were not to know it but when the storm had abated the trail of damage was the worst in living memory. Legend has it that it was not the Coxswain, Jack Crocombe, who took the initiative but the 2nd Coxswain, George Richards. When Mr Pedder reported that it

**The *Louisa*—the lifeboat that was hauled to a height of 1300 feet above sea level. ▶**

was impossible to send a telegram to Minehead because the lines
had blown down, it was George who said, 'Us'll take 'er overland to
Porlock.'

To a man the crew agreed. The lifeboat secretary, the Reverend
A.R. Hockly, Vicar of Lynmouth, gave the venture his official bless-
ing and so began the train of events that was to take the lifeboat to
a height of at least 1,300 feet and up and down hills so fearsome that
forty years later they were still being used by motor manufacturers
to test buses and lorries.

Very soon the lifeboatmen realised that what was needed was
horsepower—not the mechanical kind, but enough haulage capacity
to tow the ten-ton boat on her carriage up a one-in-three gradient.
Not only that but there had to be enough horses to complete the
fifteen mile journey. The men looked at each other for a moment.
Then through the noise of the gale half-a-dozen shouted the same
name. 'Tom Jones,' they cried.

Tom Jones was a famous Lynmouth character who ran the coach-
and-four to Porlock. Although the railway had recently reached
Lynton there was no other method of journeying from Lynmouth to
Porlock other than by coach. Tom Jones ran a big stable and soon
the village of Lynmouth echoed to the shouts of men and the clatter
of hooves. No-one knows exactly how many horses were harnessed
to the carriage, or how the existing harness was extended to take
anything up to twenty horses.

Somehow it was done. The darkness was pin-pointed by a myriad
of oil lanterns as a hundred men crossed the Lyndale Bridge and
took up station behind and beside the carriage. The gale blew harder
than ever and the rain lashed humans and animals alike. Then at the
foot of Countisbury Hill horses and men took the strain and the
journey up the incredibly steep first section began.

Even today motorists approaching this part of the hill from above
are warned to stop, put their vehicle in bottom gear and proceed
with the utmost caution. Horrific accidents involving heavy
transport and touring coaches used to make Countisbury Hill a
place to fear. Modern technology has now tamed the hill and accidents, like the one when a multi-wheel giant food lorry literally
somersaulted down the steepest part, are unlikely to recur. But
eighty years ago Countisbury Hill was no more than a stone-
surfaced track climbing at a dizzy angle. How a hundred men and
twenty horses inched their way to the top—a distance of at least a

mile-and-threequarters—remains a mystery to this day. Not only did they have to take the lifeboat and its carriage to the top; they had to prevent it from reversing back down the hill and in all probability causing horrible carnage.

What made these men embark on this seemingly impossible journey? John Pedder, grandson of the lifeboat signalman, says it was 'sheer enthusiasm'. But I think it was far more than that. Lynmouth has always been a unique village. For generations the turbulent sea was the one thing that bound everyone together. Family ties certainly helped, but overriding the innermost spirit of the village was a deep-rooted instinct to save life.

Years after the lifeboat was abolished a completely unofficial rescue boat would put to sea to go to the aid of small boats, pilots, reckless rock climbers and in fact everyone whose life had been placed in jeopardy by the dangerous seas around this part of the Bristol Channel shoreline. Nowhere in England do the cliffs rise higher. Monster tides and raging storms batter sea defences. On the map the Bristol Channel looks a peaceful stretch of water. In reality it is littered with hundreds of wrecks.

On the night of 15 August 1952, when one of England's greatest natural disasters unleashed millions of tons of floodwater to tear Lynmouth apart, the spirit of the Lynmouth villagers was remarkable. Despite the loss of over thirty souls a meeting was called within hours to plan the first steps towards rebuilding the shattered homes. Lynmouth became the symbol of an unconquerable spirit.

These men of the lifeboat crew did not see themselves as heroes. Neither did they believe they were doing anything remarkable. In fact when the story came out, the local newspaper devoted only two or three paragraphs to the entire episode but much more to the physical effects of the great storm and the damage to property.

The lifeboatmen were Lynmouth born and bred. There was William Richards, Richard Ridler, George Rawle, Charles Crick, Bertram Pennicott, David Crocombe, the village postman, John Ridler, Tom Pugsley and Richard Burgess. Youngest crewman was William Richards who was only nineteen.

What an experience for a young man, you might say. I had the good fortune to interview him many years ago at his little cottage between the East and West Lyn rivers. All his life he wore a seaman's navy blue guernsey. I remember him as quite a small man, rather taciturn and certainly not eager to play the hero. In fact all through the interview I was impressed by his matter-of-fact manner.

They had only done their duty, he kept telling me. There was a ship in trouble. The nearest lifeboat was stormbound. So was the Lynmouth boat. But the Lynmouth lifeboat could be taken across the moor. And that was what they decided to do.

He told me how they toiled and heaved their way up Countisbury Hill. William reckoned there were upwards of twenty horses straining every muscle. The storm was terrible. The gale ripped at their clothes and they were soon drenched to the skin. Their only illumination came from a few oil lanterns. The higher they went the worse the storm became.

At last they reached the top of Countisbury. There was a cheer and everyone thought they had conquered the worst of the journey, but they were sadly disappointed. William's memory faded out at this point. After all it had all happened some fifty years ago and in

**Launching the *Louisa* at Lynmouth . . .**

fairness to him the confusion must have grown worse as they battled with one obstacle after another.

Slowly the iron-shod carriage trundled across the stormswept moor. It was now well past midnight and the men had begun to calculate how they were going to overcome what they believed would be their next hazard—the descent of the precipitous Porlock Hill—with its hairpin bends and 1-3 gradient.

But they temporarily forgot about the horrors of Porlock Hill when they got to a spot known as Ashton Gate. Here the moorland track became so narrow that it was impossible to negotiate with twenty horses, a ten-ton load and a crowd of men. The crew stared in dismay. How were they to get the *Louisa,* to give her her official title, along ths narrow sunken section?

Then someone had a flash of inspiration. As part of her equipment the lifeboat carried a set of skids, presumably for launching her down a sandy beach. The system was to put the skids under each of

. . . with Countisbury Hill in the background.

the wheels, push the carriage a few feet along the skids, then repeat
the process. This was difficult enough in the daytime, but in the
inky blackness with no idea whatsoever of the kind of heather and
bog that lay ahead, it was seemingly impossible.

Somehow or other, like every obstacle on this nightmare journey,
human effort prevailed. Painfully they inched their way across the
open common. Some mathematical crewman kept a tally. In all they
moved the skids 880 times. After what seemed hours they were able
to rejoin the narrow road. Then at last someone spotted a few
candle-lit windows far below. 'Tiz Porlock,' they shouted to each
other.

Then began the most horrifying part of the journey. Whereas they
had heaved and strained to get up Countisbury Hill, now the
problem was to haul back on the ropes to stop the massive load
which towered above them from running away. Obviously they had
to unharness the horses. They belonged to Tom Jones and had to be
guarded from any harm or danger. If the boat and her carriage had
overrun the team of horses the result would have been catastrophic.

After an hour's agonising work the carriage arrived safely at the
last bend right at the bottom of Porlock Hill. The drag ropes had
somehow or other held. Then to the dismay of the exhausted men
they found their way blocked by a cottage wall. Try as they might
they could not steer the carriage round this obstacle. There was only
one thing for it: knock the wall down. To the consternation of the old
lady who lived in the cottage the wall disappeared before her eyes as
the crew attacked it with the same axes that they had used to hack
their way across the narrow moorland route.

It was 6 a.m. when they arrived at Porlock village—eight hours
after they had started from Lynmouth. Even then the crew had to
take a roundabout journey past the back of Porlock Church before
they could make for the beach at Porlock Weir and at 8 a.m. launch
the lifeboat.

Once clear of Porlock Bay the open lifeboat which had looked so
huge on its carriage was quickly reduced to size by the storm force
gale which was still blowing with only slightly less ferocity. The
men strained at the oars and eventually reached the *Forest Hall*
utterly weary and practically exhausted.

Triumph was mixed with bitter wonderment. Had it all been
worth it? The *Forest Hall*, bound for Genoa, was intact apart from a
shattered rudder-head. Both anchors were down. Somewhere out in

the murk, the Liverpool tug *Jollife* was standing by and at dawn she re-appeared. Soon, another tug, the *Sarah Jollife* reached the *Forest Hall*. Once the crew had got a fresh line aboard, the danger virtually disappeared and it was just a question of making for Barry.

Prudently, Jack Crocombe put half his crew aboard the *Forest Hall* and the Lynmouth lifeboat then escorted the casualty into harbour. Twenty-four hours after leaving Lynmouth the lifeboat and her crew were back in their home port, Jack having got a welcome tow from a passing steamer.

There is no record of a heroes' welcome. The *Forest Hall,* once her rudder-head had been repaired, proceeded on voyage to Genoa. Lynmouth's lifeboat crew were back at their respective jobs on Monday morning. As a reward each crewman received £5 which was in fact quite a handsome sum of money. The launching party shared £27 5s 6d. But there was one other detail. The Porlock cottage wall had to be repaired and this would have left the brave lifeboatmen in debt had not the owners of the *Forest Hall* contributed £75.

# THE ROYAL NAVAL COLLEGE, DARTMOUTH

*ERIC J. GROVE joined the History Department at BRNC Dartmouth in 1971 and has been Deputy Head of Strategic Studies and International Affairs since 1982. He is author of a number of books and articles on military and naval subjects and was co-author of the most recent history of the College. His main research at present is into the history of the post-1945 Royal Navy.*

No collection of Devon Sea Stories would be complete without reference to Dartmouth, for Dartmouth has contributed significantly to both the story of Devon and the Royal Navy.

The training of new entry naval officers came to Dartmouth on 30 September 1863 when HMS *Britannia* was towed to her mooring by Mill Creek on the River Dart. Since 1859 she had been the static training ship in which officer cadets, boys entering about the age of thirteen, received their first introduction to navigation, seamanship, mathematics, drawing and the other subjects of which a knowledge was required before they went to sea as midshipmen.

The idea of giving such a course was a new one; it had originated in 1857 in Portsmouth on board the rather smaller ship *Illustrious*. The more spacious *Britannia* had been forced to leave the ancient naval base because of worries about both the physical and moral health of the cadets. Her first new home had been Portland but the exposed roadstead there had soon made life unbearable. Dartmouth was chosen, not for any special Royal Navy connection, but because it offered a sheltered anchorage with easy access to the shore, and suitable land for playing fields.

To extend the accommodation the two decker *Hindostan* arrived in 1864. She was moored ahead of the *Britannia*, connected by a

The scene at Dartmouth from 1869 to 1905 with the
fifth HMS *Britannia* (left) and the third HMS
*Hindostan* (right) forming the Britannia training
establishment. The two static hulks were linked by a
gangway, floating under which is the cadets' steam-
heated winter swimming pool. The site of the future
college is the hillside.

gangway. Despite falling entries, accommodation still proved insufficient and in 1869 a replacement *Britannia* appeared in the shape of a large new 'wooden wall' made obsolete while still under construction by the ironclad revolution in warship design. Originally named *Prince of Wales*, she was completed as a training hulk and never went to sea under her own power. Also in 1869 the course of training was extended from fifteen months to two years.

It was hoped that the new accommodation would improve the health of the cadets but epidemics of smallpox and scarlet fever soon demonstrated that all was still not entirely satisfactory. In 1875 the Rice Committee recommended that a college be built on

**Britannia Royal Naval College today. The original buildings are in the front. Behind the clock tower is the extra block of 1907 and at the back the huge new block opened in 1918.**

shore and another committee under another admiral, Wellesley this time, set about trying to find a suitable spot. After consideration of a number of other places the members of the committee came back to Dartmouth as their first choice, 'admirable . . . in all respects, possessing every requisite . . .'

The Dartmouth location had by now become an item of considerable public controversy and it was easier to leave things as they were. Financial considerations confirmed political ones and the next twenty years passed by with things little changed on the Dart. The Luard Committee's recommendations of 1885, that the Solent or Portsmouth was a better place for the *Britannia,* were ignored, but in the 1890s simultaneous crises in both discipline and health re-opened the question of a college on shore. Supervision of the cadets in *Britannia* was somewhat lax. It was in the hands of 'corporals', naval police, whose general reputation for corruption was notorious. The ship's lieutenants had little to do and it was said that they relieved each other on the platforms of Paddington Station! In this atmosphere bullying was rife and, despite a somewhat enlightened official system of discipline, life for some cadets could be made so unpleasant that they ran away.

Disquiet became public and two things were done. First each term of cadets was put under the supervision of a lieutenant. This 'term officer' system was the origin of the system of direct supervision still in use at today's College. A second result was to raise the question once more of a college on shore. This seemed an even more urgent requirement when a very serious epidemic of measles and pneumonia broke out in *Britannia* in early 1895. Three cadets died and the Admiralty were moved to begin discussions by the end of the year. It was duly announced in March 1896 that a college was to be built at Dartmouth. The scheme of training was to be changed too. Cadets would enter a little older, at age fourteen to fifteen, and the four terms would be shortened to around thirteen weeks each.

In fact, the process of buying the land was already under way. Legal complications held things up and it took more than two years to obtain title. Work then began on the foundations and terraces on the commanding hillside site. Tenders were then requested for the main buildings and that of Higgs and Hill, of £220,600, was accepted in April 1900. The architect was one of the most notable of the age, Aston Webb, designer of the new frontage of Buckingham Palace. The architecture was denounced by contemporary critics as 'a cross between a workhouse and a stable' but to modern eyes the resulting building is a fine piece of Late-Victorian/Edwardian architecture in the grand manner. Money and authority were provided by the Acts raising massive naval loans to fund the shore infrastructure of a fleet that was undergoing unprecedented peacetime expansion to maintain the recently defined 'two power standard'.

As work progressed the *Britannia*'s sickness problems reasserted themselves with an especially serious influenza epidemic. First priority was, therefore, the new hospital which was opened in 1902. The same year, King Edward VII laid the foundation stone of the main building. He had sent his sons to the *Britannia* a quarter of a century before, beginning a tradition of Royal students that has continued to the present.

The year 1902 was even more important. At the year's end a major reform of officer training was announced. As well as criticising the *Britannia*'s location the committees of the previous thirty years had called for major changes in the scheme of training carried out on board and in the fleet. There was too much cramming, too much rote learning, not enough attention to new technology, no real attempt to develop the boys intellectually to face the challenges of a new naval environment. Once they left the *Britannia*, midshipmen often learned little at sea. The new Second Sea Lord, Admiral Sir John Fisher, had the force of character to get things moving at last. In co-operation with some of the leading contemporary educationalists, he designed a new scheme, announced in a memorandum that appeared over the name of Lord Selborne, the First Lord.

The new scheme introduced one entry for officers of all specialisations, with a common period of training and education, the first four years being spent in colleges on shore. Cadets would join between the ages of twelve and thirteen and spend twelve terms being educated in science, engineering, mathematics, history, English and modern languages. What was being planned was a unique system of secondary education in the applied sciences, leavened by the 'modern' humanities, that was in many ways ahead of its time.

Fisher, typically, wished to get the scheme running as soon as possible, but there were serious problems. The new 'Britannia Royal Naval College' was still two years from completion and, moreover, was too small. While it was completed and extensions added, a new college was built with remarkable speed in the grounds of the late Queen Victoria's house at Osborne on the Isle of Wight. It opened in 1903, and for two years the old and new schemes continued side by side. Indeed, the new College at Dartmouth was kept closed until the Selborne Scheme cadets were ready to move up. Extraordinary measures were taken to make sure that there was as little *Britannia* influence as possible up the hill. So that the new scheme cadets should not be overwhelmed, the three existing *Britannia* terms were shipped off to Bermuda in cruisers to complete their training there! As a result, when the new College finally did open in September 1905, the fifteen year old 'St Vincents' from Osborne outnumbered the single term of 'Hawkes' of similar age who were the penultimate term of the old scheme.

By the summer of 1907 the College was fully operational with six terms, 359 cadets, all of the Selborne scheme. Some measures were being taken to provide more accommodation in what were still inadequate buildings. The work of eradicating *Britannia* influence went on too and even its name had disappeared from the College's title. It was now plain 'Royal Naval College, Dartmouth', with the ship name HMS *Espiegle,* a gunboat that had taken up Hindostan's vacant berth. *Britannia* herself remained as ratings' quarters, her name taken by a modern battleship.

The staff of the College was part naval and part civilian, the latter in far greater numbers than in the old *Britannia.* The headmaster was the man who had started Osborne, Cyril Ashford. He controlled a staff of twenty six masters and four naval instructors. The Captain was in overall charge and had a naval staff of twenty nine officers, who supervised the cadets out of teaching hours and ran the College administration. In its early days Dartmouth seems to have been a most dynamic and progressive institution. It even produced a Nobel Prize winning scientist, Professor Lord Blackett, who entered in 1912.

By that time individual terms were beginning to total seventy cadets but it was still not enough to officer the expanding navy required by Anglo-German naval rivalry. In 1913 a rival scheme of 'Special Entries' was begun, training boys from public schools in a cruiser. Plans were also made to increase Dartmouth terms to 110, a move that would necessitate a doubling of the College's accommodation. In the Summer of 1914 work began on a massive new

**1915: On receipt of the terse order 'Mobilize',
the cadets gather their sea chests to join the fleet.**

extension which, as well as providing more classroom and living accommodation, also allowed better laboratories to be built, as well as a proper masters' common room. The design was carried out in Aston Webb's office but he seems to have had little to do with the new work and the somewhat uninspired new block, when completed, ruined the appearance of the College as seen from afar.

In August 1914 the life of the original Dartmouth came to an abrupt end. The Captain received the terse order, 'Mobilise', and, within hours, the cadets were on their way to their war billets in some of the older, and, as it turned out, more vulnerable ships of the Reserve Fleet. For the rest of the war the College continued to operate but there were considerable fluctuations in course length that hindered the attainment of the previous high standards. The supervision of the superannuated officers also left a lot to be desired and some rather unpleasant disciplinary practices entered the Dartmouth tradition as senior boys were given more latitude to dominate the others.

In 1917-18 the new buildings came into use and with the end of the war the entries of officers were reduced by half. Osborne was proving unhealthy thanks to its rapid and rather inadequate construction. The obvious solution was to close the junior college and concentrate all cadets at Dartmouth. They would all fit in if a term was dropped from the course. This was done in 1920-21 and the new Dartmouth settled down once more to a regular routine. Boys now came to Dartmouth at thirteen—the age of entry had been raised just before the war—and spent eleven terms at the College moving from gunroom to gunroom around the building. In 1921 the idea of interchangeability of executive and engineer officers was dropped and all Dartmouth cadets who wished were allowed to specialise as executive officers. The amount of engineering in the syllabus was greatly reduced. The staff now totalled fifty-five masters and thirty-nine officers.

As if to symbolise the new system and some of its slightly more old fashioned features the College's name reverted to *Britannia*. It had been *Pomone* after the old cruiser hulk that had replaced *Espiegle* in 1910 but, at the end of 1922, *Pomone* herself was towed away. The old *Britannia* hulk had long since gone, in 1916, for her copper bottom to be made into shell cases. So a small launch from Osborne officially became *Britannia* as the 'ship' upon whose books the College's naval staff were borne.

Despite Ashford's unhappiness with some of the latest developments many see the period that now began as the classic age of Dartmouth's history. Changes were few between 1921 and 1937, the major one being the arrival of a new headmaster in 1927, E.W.E. Kempson, an ex HM Inspector of schools. Naturally Kempson introduced academic improvements recommended by the Inspectors after their 1926 visit, notably the introduction of special Alpha classes for the brighter cadets. But, as the 1930s wore on, criticism of the College mounted. The number of cadets dropped as financial stringencies became more severe and the economic viability of Dartmouth was seriously questioned. By 1934 there were only thirty-six masters and twenty officers looking after 368 cadets.

Parents were preferring the Special Entry and one reason was the rather strange term system at Dartmouth whereby one term was forbidden to have contact with any other. This was changed in 1937 when the entire establishment was reorganised into six 'Houses' on public school lines with cadets of different ages, except the very youngest, in each house. The most junior boys had a house of their own. The houses were called after the Admirals whose names had previously been borne by the individual terms. The house system with house officers survives to this day in the modern Dartmouth, except that the adult officers under training are formed into 'Divisions' with 'Divisional Officers'. Even three of the names—'St Vincent', 'Blake' and 'Hawke'—remain also, having been used as term names since 1905-6.

As war clouds gathered the rival Special Entries appeared at Dartmouth in 1939 to do their professional training on shore instead of in a ship required for active service. When war actually broke out there was no repetition of 1914 and the College got fuller still as more Special Entries arrived and the passing out term of Dartmouth's own cadets was unable to get their sea training either. The College soon acquired important administrative roles as the

**On 18 September 1942 German fighter bombers hit the college. Only one person was killed but damage was extensive.**

The Queen, as Princess Elizabeth, at Dartmouth in
1939—one of her first early meetings with Prince Philip.

Captain took over control of the port in Dartmouth. WRNS officers
and ratings began to appear to man the offices. This process continued until 18 September 1942, when disaster struck in the shape
of FW190 fighter bombers coming in over Torbay. Happily term
had not started and casualties were limited to one unfortunate
WRNS rating killed by one of the bombs.

The new headmaster, J.W. Stork, now had the job of arranging
the College's evacuation. First, the junior boys were sent away to an
orphanage in Bristol that was soon dignified with the title *HMS
Bristol*. The four senior terms remained at first but it was decided to
convert the College into a combined operations training centre and
concentrate *Britannia* at a new location at Eaton Hall in Cheshire.

This was duly done by February 1943 and the College buildings became, in their new incarnation, first HMS *Dartmouth II* and then HMS *Effingham*. After only a year in their new role the buildings then passed to the US Navy who used them as an advanced amphibious base for the Normandy landings.

Not until September 1946 did HMS *Britannia* with its 'Dart' (Dartmouth Entry) and 'Benbow' (Special Entry) cadets return to its old home. The buildings had been re-furbished with greatly improved library and laboratory facilities and still more building work was in progress. Shortly after this the government decided to alter the age of 'Dart' entry from thirteen to sixteen. The aim was to take Dartmouth out of the standard 'Public School' system and democratise the officer corps. Fees for boarding and tuition were to be abolished. The first sixteen entries arrived in September 1948, and the last boys to enter at thirteen joined in May 1949.

The age sixteen entry scheme did not prove very successful. It attracted some very able boys from grammar and elementary schools but the Admiralty were soon showing disquiet about the low numbers from the public schools, who preferred their own 'Special Entry' at eighteen. The low birth rate of the 1930s complicated matters further and by 1953 there were only 247 cadets of both entries. Large parts of the College, including some newly completed sections, were closed.

Already major changes were in the wind. In 1953 a Committee on Cadet Entry produced majority and minority reports on the way forward. The majority wished to turn Dartmouth into a kind of naval boarding school with a reversion to entry at thirteen but the minority report recommended going eventually for a standard entry for all at eighteen. The Admiralty decided to do the latter immediately and the Committee on Officer Structure and Training (COST) formed in 1954 was given as its first task the drawing up of a suitable scheme. It recommeded setting up a 'Naval Academy' in the existing Dartmouth buildings which would provide a course lasting in all twenty-eight months, including time spent at sea in an attached Dartmouth Training Squadron (DTS).


**◄ Royal connections with Dartmouth have been strong.
The Prince of Wales was a member of a Graduate
Officers' professional training course in 1971.**

The College began to be transformed as the first 'COST' entries arrived in 1955. School dormitories and classrooms became college single cabins and tutorial rooms. The masters became lecturers. Mr Stork was transformed into the first Director of Studies. The staff, especially the naval staff, was greatly increased. By summer of 1957 there were fifty-seven officers and forty-two lecturers looking after 171 cadets and 419 midshipmen, as the more senior officers under training were now rated. Again a change of name symbolised the transformation. In 1953 the commissioning of the Royal Yacht *Britannia* had necessitated the College acquiring its latest, and up to the present, definitive appellation, Britannia Royal Naval College, HMS *Dartmouth.*

The COST scheme had a short life. In 1958 a new committee chaired by Sir Keith Murray toyed with the idea of restoring entry at thirteen but, instead, produced a radically changed eighteen entry scheme; a year as a cadet at Dartmouth and in DTS, a year at sea as a midshipman, a year back at Dartmouth for university-like education as a sub-lieutenant. With some amendment the scheme was adopted and Dartmouth embarked on a happy decade with a generally successful system. Other groups of officers began to arrive to diversify the College scene. 'Upper Yardmen'—able young ratings promoted to officer training—who had already briefly been at Dartmouth from 1951 to 1955, now returned permanently.

Supplementary List aircrew officers arrived in 1960, Supplementary List seamen the following year, SL engineers later still. Instructor officers under training came in 1962 and increasingly large numbers of Commonwealth and foreign officers began to arrive also. Officers who had been to university, or who were going, came for naval training. By the mid 1960s there were almost 700 officers under training of various kinds being supervised by fifty-four officers and thirty-four lecturers. The decline in numbers of lecturers reflected the increasing emphasis on short courses of professional naval training in subjects such as seamanship, operations and warfare, navigation and supply administration and management.

After this all-time peak, numbers then began a downward slide. This was partly due to the growth in the practice of sending officers to university. Indeed, for a time in the late sixties, it seemed as if the College would lose its academic role completely as various alternatives, all abortive, were mooted. The 'Murray Scheme', however,

46

was doomed. It was replaced in 1972 by a 'Naval College Entry'
that is the present basic system for officers not intended for outside
university education. Naval College Entries of the General and
Supplementary lists enter Dartmouth for a term of 'General Naval
Training'. They then spend the following term in the Dartmouth
Training Ship—HMS *Fearless* or *Intrepid*—and then return for
either one term (SL) or two terms (GL) of academic instruction in
science, mathematics, engineering, strategic studies and sometimes
modern languages or economics in addition. Alternatively, if they
are engineers, they leave after DTS to do their degrees at the Royal
Naval Engineering College at Manadon; a few of various specialisations are nominated to other universities. To mark the change the
old rank of cadet was abolished. Normally, NCE officers under
training are midshipmen throughout their time at the College.

A visitor would be struck, however, by the variety of ranks and
types of OUT (officer under training) in today's Dartmouth. There are

**The Queen watches as Prince Philip plants a tree at
the passing-out parade of Prince Andrew who was a
member of '93 Flight' in 1979-80.**

many other entries in addition to those described above. To add to the arrivals of the 1960s, the 1970s brought three main new groups: the Special Duties Candidates of St George Division, senior rates selected for promotion; 'Short Introductory Courses' of doctors, dentists, chaplains and nurses (the first female officers under training came in 1973); and in 1976, the WRNS officer cadets of Talbot Division. The atmosphere of the College had decisively altered by 1980. Instead of an extended period of training and one basic scheme there were now a whole range of entry schemes, several courses lasting not more than one term at Dartmouth and sometimes even less.

Thus, in all its confusing diversity, we leave the 'BRNC' of the 1980s. The naval cutbacks announced in 1981 have had some effect. Numbers of students had been reduced from 509 at the end of 1980 to 245 by the middle of 1983, although the latter figure was up to 363 again by the end of 1983, almost the original 'full college' total of 1907. Despite all the changes, the staff, academic and naval—thirty-one and fifty-five respectively—try to maintain the best of the old Dartmouth traditions, while meeting the needs of a dynamic naval world. They can only draw instructive inspiration from the finer achievements of Dartmouth's past.

**The Norwegian steamship** *Sjofna* **ashore south of  Knaps Longpeak.**

# THE 'SJOFNA' SERVICE

*MICHAEL NIX settled in North Devon twelve years ago and has become well-known as a coastal historian, an interest that developed from painting expeditions in the Hartland area. In 1980 he co-established a Museum at Hartland Quay only yards from the Atlantic Ocean and more recently has written articles and books concerning the North Devon coastline.*

A few old salts in the coastal parish of Hartland, North Devon, will, with an almost imperceptible smile, amicably announce that history really begins on 17 November 1962. Any event before this date is to them of little significance, is, in their jargon, pre-GR—or to the better informed and, of course, more discerning of historians, pre-*Green Ranger*. Whether they have a *cause célèbre* sufficient for the nation to change its calendar is somewhat dubious but what is not doubted is their pride in the Hartland Life-Saving Apparatus Company. The role of the Company in the rescuing of the crew of the stricken Royal Fleet Auxiliary tanker *Green Ranger* is part of one of those epic narratives which has rightly established itself amongst the South West's great sea stories.

About to enter the outer reaches of the Bristol Channel, the 3,299-ton *Green Ranger*, bound for South Wales for a refit, was slipped from her tow off Hartland Point by the master of the tug *Caswell* who, in a north-westerly gale gusting force 10, feared the loss of both vessels. On a violent lee shore and without power, the 355-foot long vessel wallowed helplessly onto the prominent, saw-toothed reef of Gunpath a few miles to the south, stranding seven frightened dockyard workers on the bridge.

Coxswain Cann of the Appledore lifeboat, *Louisa Ann Hawker*, gallantly manoeuvring between a deadly sandstone *cheval-de-frise* and the ship's forbidding grey bows, was frustrated for more than a quarter of an hour in his endeavours to attract any obvious response from those on board. His withdrawal into safer waters meant the life-saving attempt was now to be entrusted to landsmen from Hartland, who, having clambered down sheer 400-foot cliffs in driving rain and sleet and carrying between them over a ton of equipment, were eventually to establish a communication between ship and shore by rocket line. All on board were safety landed by breeches buoy.

For his bravery Coxswain Cann received the RNLI silver medal and the Hartland LSA team, led by greengrocer Douglas Jeffery, was awarded the nationally coveted Ministry of Transport Wreck Service Shield. Nor was this the first occasion the men from Hartland had been so honoured.

On 24 November 1944 the Company had similarly distinguished itself during the rescue of nineteen men from the twenty-six-year old Norwegian steamship *Sjofna*, ashore about three quarters of a mile to the south of Knaps Longpeak where the *Eilianus* and *Cambalu* still protruded their rusting remains at low tide. In 1911, nineteen

**'The North Devon coastline is majestic, at times awesome . . .'**

years after its formation on 1 April 1892, following the disastrous loss of the SS *Uppingham* on Longpeak in which eight men had drowned, it had won for itself a European reputation when seventeen were extricated from the Belgian steamship *Cingetorix*. She had run ashore in thick fog three quarters of a mile below Hartland Quay. In the intervening years, with the exception of assistance given to the crews of the *Clipper* at rough anchor off Speke's Mill Mouth in 1895 and the *Rosalia* hard aground within 200 yards of the Coastguard Station at Hartland Quay in 1904, the Company's call-outs had generally involved cliff rescue work and standing by vessels in distress. Now they were to be challenged by what some observers and participants have described as Hartland's most arduous and dangerous rescue mission.

Early morning on the 24th had found the *Sjofna*, carrying a cargo of 500 tons of bagged china clay from Fowey to Larne, thickly blanketed by heavy rain squalls and dense fog, visibility reduced to a mere 50 yards. Engine trouble and high seas were relentlessly edging her into white broken water, a natural pulverising machine, beneath 350-foot cliffs. It would have been suicidal to have launched any of the ship's boats. The master, Captain Hovden and his crew, which included three British anti-aircraft gunners, found shelter on a water-drenched bridge, powerful seas breaking fully over the ship.

The responses of the life-saving organisations were rapid and well-organised. At 3 a.m. the Clovelly lifeboat, the *City of Nottingham*, was launched with the aid of some of the women of the village, their menfolk, in many cases, being away fighting a more dangerous adversary, in terms of lives lost, than the sea. In Hartland the LSA Company was being summoned by signal rocket and by the daughter of one of its members. At 3.30 a.m. the 61-foot, twin-screw Padstow lifeboat *Princess Mary*, the largest boat in the RNLI fleet, began a long and difficult service with a hard 28-mile haul to the wreck. Fifteen minutes later the blue and red painted, four-wheeled rocket waggon with its rockets, ropes and breeches buoy stowed on board, left its little stone-constructed house on the cliff head above Hartland Quay.

At 5.30 a.m. the *City of Nottingham* located the *Sjofna*, now broadside onto the shore and an hour later was joined by the *Princess Mary*. On the coast road the rocket waggon, towed for the first time on service by a tractor, trundled slowly on towards Welcombe Mouth. In making his way to the ship, the tractor driver

had driven, according to one reliable eye-witness account, within inches of the cliff edge.

Soon after first light, acting-coxswain—normally second mechanic —William Orchard of the *Princess Mary* decided to anchor outside the breakers and drop stern first towards the *Sjofna*. Large seas rushed in and over the boat. A lifeboatman fell, injured. Every breaking wave crest was challenged with throttles to the twin 80 horse-power engines thrust full forward, easing the strain on the anchor cable.

Falling astern in the troughs, the Padstow lifeboat was gradually brought within pistol-line range. Two lines snaked across the ship. Neither could be reached by the crew. Selecting a fresh position to bring him down closer to the bridge, William Orchard again entered the white maelstrom, the lifeboat's stern now smashing onto the sea bed with loud cracks audible to those assembled on shore.

At times the *Princess Mary* appeared to rear up near vertical yet the coxswain's cool courage and resolute resolve was rewarded, after a second attempt, by a quickly rigged breeches buoy securing its first man. A further six were dragged through the sea before the

**William Orchard (left) acting-coxswain of the Padstow lifeboat anchored outside the breakers and dropped stern first towards the *Sjofna* (far left).**

line parted. Having expended all the rocket lines William Orchard was forced to retire, collecting the Clovelly boat's line-throwing gun in anticipation of a further attempt.

The lorry-borne LSA team had departed Hartland ahead of its waggon and at about 5 a.m. the men began assembling on a cliff which one rescuer was later to describe, perhaps a little euphemistically, as 'very nasty'. Manhandling equipment over the cliff face in the dark and against a strong west-south-westerly wind was a laborious and formidable job. On a ledge part way down the apparatus was erected and a rocket fired but the wind curved it away from the wreck. The missile fell short.

Not until about 12.30 p.m. was it possible for a communication to be effected with the vessel and only then after a further nine rockets were expended. First to be landed was one of the three gunners who manned the stern-mounted Oerlikon and the Lewis guns on the wings of the bridge. Then near disaster as the endless whip used to pull the breeches buoy back and forth snagged and fouled in rocks to the north of the beach. A seaman, the oldest member of the ship's company, nearly drowned as the breeches buoy lurched erratically in the pulsating gulf between the ship's side and the foreshore. Men waded out towards him only to be swept back again, their war-issue great coats impeding movement and threatening to drag them under.

Realising the difficulties, sixteen-year-old Bude boy Peter Herbert, today a sea captain, and thirty-eight-year-old Coastguard Station Officer George Pawson, stripped to their underwear and, using the whip to the breeches buoy to steady themselves, tenaciously gripped an undeflected course to the mariner. A knife passed to Peter Herbert by the Coastguardsman severed the rope and the hapless survivor was dragged clear of the sea and given first-aid treatment. The young hero Herbert, bitterly cold, was incredulous to discover that, while saving the sailor's life, someone had stolen his clothes.

The apparatus was again made ready. The eleventh and final projectile, its 250-fathom Italian hemp line paid out from the canted stout deal box, failed to gain height and behaving as one of Congreve's rockets at Waterloo described a gently arcing trajectory before smashing its way through the wheelhouse. Captain Hovden's leg splintered open and the fur of a terrified ship's cat ignited. Horrified hands rushed to their aid. Others seized the rocket line, hauled in the whip ready rove through the tail block and attached it to the starboard Lewis gun mounting.

Although neap tides prevented the crew from wading ashore easier beach conditions facilitated the use of the 3-inch hawser on which the breeches buoy could be suspended from a traveller block. The remainder of the crew were landed along with two dogs and, of course, the smouldering moggy. 'Gran' O'Donnell from Hartland freely supplied both rescuers and rescued with hot food and drink, as did neighbouring residents and visiting WVS. Captain Hovden was, as gently as the boulder-strewn beach permitted, carried to Strawberry Water, Welcombe, and Peter Herbert, wrapped in a blanket, was provided with transport back to his home. The car owner initially resisted the instruction arguing a petrol shortage and a wet passenger but wartime commands were impatient of argument. The threat of having his vehicle commandeered was sufficient persuasion.

At the first opportunity the captain, after a long convalescence in hospital, hobbled his way along Queen Street, Bude, to express his gratitude to the young man who had done so much to save life. However, misfortune again bedevilled the ship's master. Peter was away at sea and having chatted to the lad's mother he lost his balance, toppled off his crutches and fractured an arm.

The ship's cat was luckier. Renamed 'Jeannie' she was adopted by the LSA's Number One, Lewis Littlejohns, who had actually fired the rocket that had set her alight. Peter Herbert was well satisfied with a plethora of clothing coupons, a reward, at a time of wartime rationing, far more acceptable than a medal. A letter from the Chief Inspector of Coastguards commented on his 'seamanlike conduct' which 'assisted materially in saving lives which might otherwise have been lost'.

For the bravest act of life-saving of the year by a lifeboatman William Orchard won the Miss Maud Smith Award for courage. The RNLI rewarded him with their silver medal and John Murt, second coxswain, and John Rokahr, motor mechanic, received the Institution's thanks on vellum.

The Hartland LSA team, of course, were gratified with the presentation of the Ministry of Transport Shield. They are still the only Company in North Devon to have possessed it. It is a reminder of both the bravery of the rescuers and the treacherous nature of this coast.

**Wreckage of the *Sjofna*. 'Salvage gangs sliced
her into pieces and sold them as scrap . . .'**

And the *Sjofna*? Salvage gangs sliced her into manageable pieces
and sold them as scrap although a few rusty remains still litter the
shoreline. Lumps of coal can be dug out of her cut down bunkers and
a few souvenirs gleaned, if you are lucky, from rock crevices. The
occasional round of ammunition causes a little consternation to
safety-conscious beachcombers but of the gallant rescue only
personal memories, official accounts and newspaper articles are
there to remind us.

# HOLLAND 1

*SANDI MARSHALL is probably best known for her work as a BBC reporter and presenter. She regularly appears on the evening magazine 'Spotlight' in the South West and recently worked as presenter of the Radio 4 programme 'Woman's Hour' and as newsreader on the lunchtime television news. She is enthusiastic about diving, sailing, gardening, painting, words and people with ideas.*

The men had been sweating all morning. Their naked backs were smeared with oil. Inch by inch they'd reclaimed the cables from the sea but still they had no real idea what they cradled. As the two cables were winched aboard, the men clamped them into place with bolts a foot long. The dead weight they carried was over a hundred tons and if a cable snapped it could lash the men from the deck.

It was a bright autumn day but the crew of RMAS *Pintail* were anxious. For them this Sunday would be the end of weeks of work —but they knew that for others there had been years of effort to get this far. The sinuous cables that ran into the sea just in front of the ship's bows carried two metal slings. Cradled carefully between them was a rusting metal hull. On the ship's monitors it was no more than a hump—a patch of light in the gloom surrounded by fish—but it had once been Britain's only submarine. The first of its kind. And she was called *Holland 1*.

The hazy form and divers' reports were all the crew knew for certain.

The divers had first been down two years earlier after a naval minesweeper confirmed that an unidentified vessel lay one hundred and eighty yards from the spot where researchers believed the submarine to be. They had submerged a remote camera and seen the famous, porpoise-shaped hull for the first time, but it was another year before recovery work began in earnest. Money was a problem and the cost of the operation could only be minimised by working it into training schedules.

So, in August 1982 the *Seaforth Clansman,* a diving vessel on charter to the Royal Navy, arrived on site off the Eddystone Rocks. On this trip, in addition to her usual gear, she carried cutting equipment and the metal straps that were to go around the submarine's belly.

A team of twenty divers then began the slow process of starting work. They went into saturation in a diving chamber in the bowels of their vessel. Their bodies slowly acclimatised to the depth at which they would have to work . . . and their minds to the prospect of being crammed into a diving chamber for up to a month at a time, living cheek by jowl with their mates.

Their lives depended on a mixture of helium and oxygen which meant they became prone to all sorts of hazards. Their bodies lost heat six times faster than usual and they were more subject to infection such as fungus and rot.

Their moves were watched on a bank of monitors and their voices listened to on speakers in the control room. A rigorous system of checks and double checks ran twenty-four hours a day to ensure their survival.

When it was time to work the first team of divers moved into the

*Pintail,* **with** *Holland 1* **hanging from the bows,
in Plymouth Sound, 1982.**

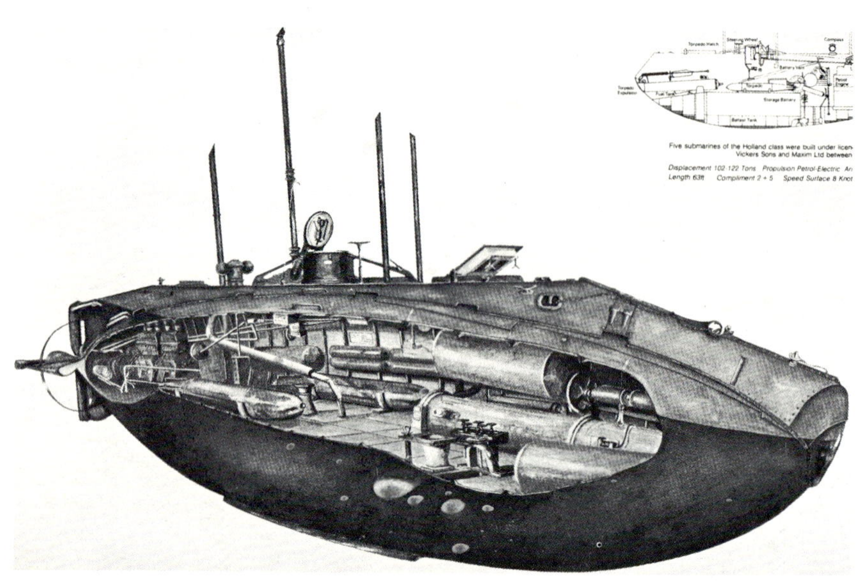


**With the help of Vickers *Holland 1* will eventually look like this again. Below, she is in Portsmouth Harbour about 1902.**

bell and were lowered into the dark sea beneath the ship. Working was a constant battle against the cold—even in suits with circulating hot water.

Below, they found the submarine was shrouded with old fish nets which they cleared with garden shears. The divers then marked up the belly to receive the metal straps. The submarine was listing ten degrees to starboard on coarse sand and the divers knew the job wouldn't be quite as bad as they'd feared. But the weather took a turn for the worse to discount that good fortune. Almost as soon as the submarine was ready for a trial lift conditions deteriorated and work was called off. Day after day the ships waited. The *Pintail* arrived, looked at the situation and buoyed off. Again they tried— but then halted, waiting for a better weather report.

When eventually the lift began, a messenger wire caught on the submarine and snapped. The area was marked off and both ships returned to Plymouth to wait for daylight. But the following morning they heard that a trawler had got too close to the area and caught its nets on the submarine. The divers had to go down again to clear it.

When their job was done, the *Pintail* took over.

So it was with bated breath that the crew of *Pintail* raised the submarine from the spot she'd occupied for seventy years. They not only raised her from the deep but also brought her, still suspended underwater, within sight of Plymouth Sound. It had been hard graft and they'd earnt their Sunday lunch. They celebrated by washing it down with a few pints of bitter

The City of Plymouth was on the skyline and the crew knew it wouldn't be long before their job was over. They had to leave the submarine on the seabed just off Drake's Island within an area marked by yellow buoys. Their only regret was that they had worked so closely with a vessel without seeing her.

They had nursed her in from the ocean on her last journey. They hadn't dared to go too slowly in case the *Pintail*'s engines objected but they couldn't go too fast for fear of damaging the cargo. They'd effectively crept in with the tide, keeping curious shipping at bay— and they'd gently lifted the *Holland 1* foot by foot as they came in.

The skipper paused in his chain smoking to reflect that the crew had worked well. It was an unusual salvage operation. They were more used to helicopters and the like on naval exercises. They deserved a perk, he thought.

It was a calm, bright day, the sky was clear and the sea was calm. He gave orders to winch up the submarine just a few more feet. As long as she didn't break surface and be exposed to the corrosive atmosphere, she was safe.

He heard a cheer go up and went to the bow. Through the surface of the water the sun picked out the glimmering shape of a conning tower smothered with clumps of limpets and sea urchins. The main body of the submarine shone more darkly—but it was all there. Those on deck pronounced themselves satisfied. 'I hope we don't bloody drop it now.'

They didn't. As dusk fell they safely lowered her onto the mud in twenty metres of water under the watchful eye of The Queen's Harbourmaster.

For the next few weeks Navy divers worked below pumping out the silt and removed most of the batteries. Without their weight the submarine would be easier to lift—and scientists were interested in testing the lead inside for radiation levels. The *Holland 1* had sunk

*Pintail,* **with** *Holland 1* **entering No.12 dock at Devonport.**

**Her conning tower with the torpedo loading hatch
opened back on it.**

before atomic tests and could give them useful information on the increase in ambient radiation.

One battery was sent back to the manufacturers too—and with glee they pronounced that it would still accept a charge.

The underwater visibility in Plymouth Sound is rarely good and the next few weeks were no exception. The silt pumping made matters worse but it was still possible to dive in the gloom. Laurie Emberson, a BBC underwater cameraman, and myself picked our day with care. The tides and the weather seemed as good as we would get and we weren't sure how much longer the submarine would stay in the relative tranquillity of the sea. We set out to take as much underwater film as we could.

Finning from one end of the hull to the other seemed to take an age but it gave us a chance to speculate how she came to be there. The bald facts were that she sank on her way to the breaker's yard just before the First World War but that's an unromantic tale. All the divers who prowled around the hull while she was off the Eddystone had remarked on the regular holes in her side which didn't

*Holland 1* **in No.12 dock at Devonport shortly after salvaging . . .**

square with her fundamentally sound condition. The more prosaic will point out that securing a submarine's conning tower from the outside is difficult. She may have shipped water through an improperly secured hatch, become unstable and been cut free by the towing vessel before they, too, foundered. But the imaginative will always prefer to think there was a more interesting tale that will never be told.

Her fascination for most people is that she was the forerunner of all submarines in the world's major navies. The United States, Russia, Japan, The Netherlands and Chile all built submarines to her design, and there isn't one other example of her type surviving today.

Her past was a curious one. She was invented by an Irish American called John Philip Holland who had the fond hope that she would prove the secret weapon that would drive the British out of Ireland. But he turned out to be a pragmatist. He ended up

64

**. . . she was then waterblasted and sprayed with
chemical preservatives.**

selling his design to the 'enemy'. However, Admiralty top brass was
less farsighted than the little Irish American. They were, frankly,
appalled. 'Its damned un-English' was one of the more printable
comments on the idea. Many of the establishment felt submariners
should be shot in times of war as pirates, but history has proved
who was the most perceptive.

This showed nowhere more clearly than in November 1982 when
*Holland 1* was berthed in a dry-dock at Devonport Dockyard.
Millions of gallons of water were pumped out before the watching
crowds and the world's press. As she broke surface it was John
Philip Holland's finest hour because he'd got it right. The submarine—although tiny beside her modern nuclear counterparts—
was the same shape. Her porpoise-like lines were designed so that
she could travel most efficiently underwater and that is the design
to which modern submarine architects have returned.

The first thing that broke surface in Devonport that day was a

Union Jack, placed there by a diver who clearly felt she shouldn't
return to port after such a lengthy dive without the proper attire.
Once the hull was visible the water seemed to run away rapidly and
she lay rather pathetically on her chocks barely filling the width of
the dock.

For the Dockyard it was a triumph. It was the first time—and
maybe the last—that they'd had to berth an unseen vessel. But the
winter days were against them. The light was failing and the tem-
perature falling. If the hull wasn't preserved within twenty-four
hours she would decay beyond repair and everyone's efforts would
have been in vain.

High pressure hoses ripped away the rust and plant life leaving

*Holland 1* **soon after arrival at the RN Submarine
Museum, Gosport, in December 1982. The hull was
cut into three sections for transportation.**

the steel gleaming like new. But before their eyes it began to yellow and the chemical teams moved in to spray the body with a substance that converted rust to metal. Soon the submarine was a thick black lump—ungainly but safe.

Next it was the turn of the chemists who had to give the all-clear before cutting work could begin. In 1901 when the *Holland 1* was first launched she carried three white mice in a cage above the engines to warn of noxious gases. In theory they had time to squeak a warning before they died. Fortunately for the cutters Devonport Dockyard boasted more sophisticated detection devices.

Cutting up the submarine was a controversial idea, rumoured to be because the Navy wouldn't allow the whole structure to be moved across playing fields next to the submarine museum at Gosport in Hampshire. The museum's curator said he didn't mind because once in pieces it would be easier for the visiting public to get inside. The purists remained unconvinced.

The three sections were hoisted from the dock by a submarine refuelling crane. They travelled rather ignominiously by road to become a showpiece at the museum. On opening day it provoked unstinted praise from Admiralty top brass whose forebears had so derided the little vessel which had pointed the way to naval warfare as we know it today.

# SIR FRANCIS DRAKE

*SARAH FOOT lives at Elm Gate, her home over-looking the River Lynher. She has contributed seven titles to the Bossiney list, her latest being* **The Cornish Countryside** *and she is currently working on* **Rivers of Cornwall.** *Formerly on the staff of* **The London Evening News,** *she writes regularly for* **The Western Morning News.**

Few British school children can have studied the history of their country in the sixteenth century without feeling a thrill of excitement at the stories of Sir Francis Drake. There were many sea-going heroes of that age but somehow Drake shone above them all and captured the imagination of British people for evermore.

*Drake he was a Devon man an' ruled the Devon seas*
*(Captain art thou sleepin' there below?)*
*Rovin' tho' his death fell, he went wi' heart of ease,*
*An dreamin' arl the time of Plymouth Hoe,*
*'Take my drum to England, hang it by the shore,*
*Strike it when the powders runnin' low,*
*If the Dons sight Devon, I'll quit the port of Heaven,*
*An drum them up the channel as we drumm'd them long ago.'*

So wrote Newbolt in the last century and hundreds of young people learning those lines felt their imaginations roused as they do to this day.

**Queen Elizabeth I went aboard the *Golden Hinde* and conferred on Drake a knighthood.** ▶

Drake's story has all the ingredients to fill us with admiration and wonder. He came from a humble background, born in the early 1540s in a cottage in a small Devon village near Tavistock. He went to sea at a very early age, had a rich and influential godfather, Lord Russell, and gained success in his voyages and the confidence of his crew when still a very young man.

He was fearless, full of ingenuity and kind and thoughtful to the men who accompanied him on his voyages as well as with his prisoners. His coolheadedness in battle became legendary while he was still alive and his strong Protestant faith was a centre point in his life. Today his adventurous spirit seems all the more admirable and extraordinary.

Although he was first and foremost a sailor he was also devoted to the town of Plymouth, of which he was Mayor from 1581-2. He was the prime mover in bringing water to Plymouth, his interest being inspired by the realisation of how much easier it would be to water a fleet in the harbour.

It was from Plymouth harbour that Drake sailed on all his famous voyages; his circumnavigation of the globe, the first accomplished by an Englishman, began and ended in Plymouth Sound. It was from here in 1588 that he set out to defeat the Spanish Armada and it was again from Plymouth that he sailed on his last voyage from which he was destined never to return, dying of dysentery and being buried at sea.

Drake had been tackling voyages of great danger for nearly twenty years before he received the Queen's recognition in 1581. It was during a visit to Deptford in London that the Queen went aboard his ship, the *Golden Hinde,* and conferred on him the honour of a knighthood. She also ordered that his ship should be preserved in memory of his own and his country's glory. When the *Golden Hinde* finally decayed, a chair made from its planks was given to the University of Oxford.

In 1587 King Philip of Spain rallied all his sea power to overthrow the fleet of his arch enemies, the English. But Drake set off with a

**◄ Drake has left behind him many a legend. He succeeded in bringing a water supply to Plymouth by bewitching a Dartmoor stream and leading it into town at the heels of his horse.**

strong contingent and sailed into the very harbour of Cadiz where he destroyed over thirty ships yet escaped unscathed. On the same voyage he wrecked many more ships, bombarded several forts and eventually captured the *St Philip,* one of the finest ships in Spain.

This kind of brazen behaviour to the threatening Spaniards appealed enormously to the vast majority of the people in Britain who welcomed him home from his conquests with great enthusiasm. On his return from one such voyage the Church of St Andrews in Plymouth was full with a Sunday evening congregation. The whisper spread through the crowd that Drake was sailing into Sutton Harbour and within minutes the church was emptied and everyone had gone to the waterfront to greet their local hero.

One has to remember the state of the warring European coun-

**This painting shows Don Pedro de Valdez surrendering his sword to Drake during the Spanish Armada.**

tries, the lack of knowledge of the geography of the world, the few and inaccurate charts, the comparative frailty of sea-going vessels at the time when Sir Francis was living to appreciate fully his extraordinary valour and insatiable desire for adventure and discovery.

His voyages were often planned so that he could seize valuable gold, jewels and silver from the rich Spanish ships which sailed constantly between Spain, Africa—to collect slaves—the West Indies and South America where vast numbers of Spaniards had emigrated. Drake, himself, was not above joining in the lucrative slave trade that the Spaniards had started. However, he was also fired by the desire to discover new sea routes and to travel right round the world.

Some called him a pirate—he preferred to be called a privateer. He wanted to feel that what he did was done for the good of his country and his Queen and the wealth he himself accumulated was always secondary. He was mistrusted by many of the men who surrounded the Queen and the court was suspicious of him since he was not a man of high birth. But again and again on returning from a trip when he might have expected the Queen's wrath for his plundering he was forgiven and congratulated and his treasures were all used to swell the coffers of the English treasury.

His famous ship the *Golden Hinde* was originally called *Pelican*. He renamed her when circumnavigating the world. He was sailing through the Straits of Magellan against heavy odds and in the most terrible storms he was ever to encounter. At one time he and his crew sailed for sixty eight days without sighting land which must have been a most alarming experience for men who were never sure about the shape of the world.

He was beset by problems on all his voyages: sickness, starvation, incredible storms which often completely scattered his ships and sometimes sank them, and the constant danger of attack both on sea and land. His faith sustained him: often before going into battle he led his men in prayer, believing implicitly in the power of God.

He was a tempestuous man by nature, of fairly small build, but with such presence and sense of honour and humour that both friends and enemies were inclined to admire him, although there were many Spaniards who were forever to hate the very sound of his name.

He was less sophisticated and not such a diplomat as his cousin and friend, John Hawkins, who did so much for his career in the early days. Hawkins' charm was legendary and he was always able to get the most from his adversaries with gentle persuasion, but Drake was ambitious and could be canny and sly though always generous. He learned to love the sound of his voice, was brilliant at rallying his men in moments of danger and his crew always served him with utter loyalty. The only time that his men were to lose courage in battle was when he was shot in the leg at Nombre de Dios. Then they forced Drake, who was bleeding profusely, to return to his ship and the planned plunder of the town did not take place.

One of his biographers, George Malcolm Thomson, wrote: 'Drake was a "card", that is to say, a man of character whom a touch of eccentricity redeemed from the commonplace.' Certainly he influenced the youth of his day. His way of life appealed to the rather wild, unruly young people of the sixteenth century and they followed him willingly to sea knowing the terrible dangers and that never, or very, very rarely, did a ship return with all its crew intact. This enormous popularity with the ordinary people was one of his greatest strengths and one which those in more lofty positions were forced to respect.

It is not surprising that with such a character and a reputation for bravery, daring, adventure and straightforward loyalty, Drake has left behind him many a legend built up on fact and some fiction. But looking back to the true stories on which the legends were built one is often confronted with facts that are even more moving and admirable than the legends they inspired. In Drake's story fact is always stronger than fiction.

The most famous part of the Drake saga is probably his drum and the legend that if it was beaten in times of trouble Drake's spirit would return to help out those in danger. When he set off around the world in 1577 Drake took with him a 'smart new drum'. When he was knighted he had his coat of arms painted on it and the drum was always beaten prior to his ship going into action. In his attack on Nombre de Dios Drake advanced 'with pikes and flaming arrows, and one trumpet and drum making a hell of a noise up the main street'. The drum is now kept at Buckland Abbey a few mile from Plymouth and once one of Drake's houses.

Legend has it that the drum beat when the German fleet surrendered in November 1918 and again at the time of Dunkirk. Nelson is supposed to have heard it when he came to be made a Freeman of the Borough, and there were those who heard the drum beat when

Napoleon was brought as a prisoner on the *Bellerophon* into Plymouth Sound. And so the drum has become part of British folk-lore to give all those in trouble new courage.

When Drake was anchored at Cape Sakar on 17 May 1587 he wrote a letter home. The first paragraph read: 'There must be a begynnying of any great matter, but the contenweing unto the end untyll it be thoroughly ffynyshed yeldes the trw glory.' From these words evolved Drake's Prayer.

In 1941 there was a collection of prayers of early times published by the Oxford University Press and the words of Drake were repro-

**Crowndale Farm, Tavistock, near the place where Drake was born.**

duced to accompany the following prayer which has become famous the world over. 'Oh Lord God, when Thou givest to Thy servants to endeavour any great matter, grant us also to know that it is not the beginning, but the continuing of the same unto the end, until it be thoroughly finished which yieldeth the true glory; through Him who for the finishing of Thy work laid down His life, our Redeemer, Jesus Christ.'

So the most famous of all Devon's nautical heroes had a character with many facets.

His strong Protestant faith, his great bravery, his love of Queen and country were mixed with his firm sense of honour and justice and the care and understanding he showed to all the men who worked with him or for him. There were always people in high positions who mistrusted him and who, from time to time, spoke out against him. They may have been jealous of him. Some thought he took too many unnecessary risks, and others thought him too authoritarian.

The fact remains that Drake lived in an age when there were many great adventurers but it is his name and the legends he inspired which remain most famous, which turn history into a thrilling experience and which inspire us all to admiration to this day. His exploits appealed to the vast majority of ordinary people in England in his own lifetime. He was a hero of his day. Yet many people now feel, as I do, when they pass his statue on the Hoe at Plymouth or in Tavistock, a thankfulness that such men of bravery and vigour were sent to colour our lives as well.

**Statue of Drake at Tavistock. 'He was a hero of his day.'** ▶

# THE TORBAY LIFEBOAT

*MONICA WYATT came to Teignmouth in 1978 and is now a senior reporter for West of England Newspapers Ltd. Her first published work was as a researcher and contributor to a guide on the public parks and botanical gardens of Europe. She is also a freelance contributor to magazines and has recently completed a volume for A. Wheaton's series 'Faith in Action'.*

The sea has helped shape the character of Devon and its heritage. In any title about Devon and the sea, reference and tribute must be given to the Royal National Lifeboat Institution, which is entirely supported by voluntary contributions.

Its lifeboats and volunteer crews go out at all hours and in all weathers to save lives. Their string of successes, the many people and craft saved, often do not catch newspaper headlines in the same way as do the disasters at sea. 'Bad news makes good news,' is a comment often made about the Press but good news *can* make good reading.

The lifeboat stations of South Devon have scores of sea stories buried in their files, stories which reveal great courage, swift and accurate reactions to difficult situations and plenty of humour, too.

The Torbay lifeboat station was established in 1866 after a severe easterly gale wrecked many sailing ships which had tried to take shelter in the bay. More than a hundred sailors were drowned and it

**Captain Barry Anderson (left) receiving a model of the *Edward Bridges* from the coxswain, Arthur Curnow. It was presented by the Torbay lifeboat crew to mark his retirement in 1983. ▶**

Left: Captain Barry Anderson,
Honorary Secretary of
Torbay lifeboat station
from 1975 to 1983.

was said one could walk all along the wreckage on the south-west side of the bay.

The person who organises the launching of the lifeboat, following it through from the first coastguard alert to the arrangement of hospital checks and overnight accommodation for the rescued, is the station's honorary secretary.

For eight years, from 1975 until November 1983, the honorary secretary was Captain Barry Anderson, CBE, JP, DL, RN. He first went to sea at the age of fourteen but now he is in his late sixties and he and his wife Gwen live in Brixham. While his 'bleeper' radio receiver stood on the mantelpiece in case of a coastguard alert, he told me about the most difficult, the most hazardous and the most unusual rescue missions in the last eight years of the *Edward Bridges,* Torbay's modern lifeboat, stationed at Brixham.

## The LYRMA: 6 December 1976

The most difficult was that of the *Lyrma.* The seven lifeboat crew—including fishermen, builders and postmen—saved ten lives when they went out in a force-ten wind at one o'clock in the morning.

When the Torbay lifeboat set out to help the *Lyrma,* a vessel with its radar and steering gear out of action and its cargo shifting, it met waves that measured 40 feet from trough to crest. The high sea was covered with spume and spray and at times the lifeboat was partially airborne. Many of the crewmen were seasick.

The *Lyrma* was out of control and moving round in a circle. At each wave the whole propeller came out of the water and the 2nd Coxswain, Mr Keith Bower, asked for helicopter assistance. One arrived from the R.F.A. *Engadine,* 20 miles away, and a man was lowered. In the gale he began to swing like a pendulum and his wire became tangled with the ship's ropes. He was injured but lifted to safety.

By then it was 3.30 a.m. The *Lyrma* had stopped and its cargo was shifting to the leeward side. Because of the flying spray and the swaying motion of the ship, the crew did not want to use the in-

◄ **The Torbay lifeboat returns after rescuing the crew of the *Lyrma.***

flatable liferaft. It was up to Mr Bower, a thirty-year-old married man with two children and on duty that night as Coxswain, to react to the situation within seconds.

The lifeboat made six runs alongside the *Lyrma*, in which seven men and one woman jumped into the arms of the lifeboat men on the foredeck. The crew virtually held on to the foredeck's rails with one hand and used the other to grasp the survivors as they jumped down. During the last of the six runs, the *Lyrma* came down on to the lifeboat, bending the metal support stanchions to 45 degrees. The last two on the *Lyrma* managed to use their liferaft and were then rescued by the lifeboat.

It is one thing to rescue the crew of a stricken vessel, sometimes quite another to bring them all safely to shore. The lifeboat made its way back but the waves were still huge and the visibility as poor as before.

Keith Bower stayed on the upper deck so that he could watch the waves and judge his speed, but he insisted that the rest of his crew

**The crew of the *Lyrma* come ashore . . .**

and the *Lyrma*'s survivors stay in the wheelhouse with the doors tightly shut. Keeping those doors shut is the one essential to ensure that the boat rights itself if it capsizes. That way, he knew that if the worst happened, everyone—except himself—would be safe.

His instinctive courage and good judgement earned him an RNLI gold medal and the rest of the crew a bronze medal, with special commendations for the navigator, John Dew, and the 2nd Coxswain, John Hunkin.

All the *Lyrma* crew went to hospital for a check-up and apart from shock suffered no injuries.

Two years later the crewmen of the *Edward Bridges* had one of their most frightening experiences ever as they returned to Brixham after a launch.

## The LESLIE H: 19 February 1978

After rescuing the two crew on the *Leslie H*, a pilot cutter which set out from Brixham harbour in heavy onshore seas and 50 knot winds,

**. . . from the Torbay lifeboat—the *Edward Bridges***

the Torbay lifeboat was hit by a freak 40-foot wave with a 12-foot curling crest.

The rescue had gone well because the lifeboat crew had been 'tipped off' in good time. Deputy launching authority Mr Tony Smith had seen the *Leslie H* leave harbour and the crew was ready to launch. Sure enough, a mayday call was received and within three minutes the *Edward Bridges* was on its way. Within another 23 minutes the two crew had been rescued and the *Leslie H* was in tow.

Then came the freak 40-foot wave, smashing against the lifeboat and flinging her on her beam ends. She went so far over that the Coxswain, Mr George Dyer, who was on the upper bridge, went into the sea, managing to kick off his sea boots on the way. Mr John Ashford, one of the lifeboat crew, was swept overboard. Five gallons of sea water went into the port engine sump, the mast bent six degrees, the radar trans-ceiver filled with sea water and the blue light topping the mast smashed.

Just a mile away, observers on Berry Head cliffs watched as the wave hit the boat, threw spray 90 feet up into the air and covered the boat with foam.

Within seconds the boat had righted herself and the crewman in the sea was pulled aboard by 'wiggling' out the tow rope to him. The seas became steeper and the decision had to be made to leave the pilot cutter a derelict. It now lies beneath the Berry Head cliffs.

The moment when the boat went over 110 degrees was one of the most frightening the lifeboat crew had ever faced, yet later they were able to say that they had more confidence than before in their Arun-class boat. Repeated training exercises of 'man overboard' and other rules had also proved invaluable.

Captain Anderson, as honorary secretary, received a score of congratulatory phone calls for the crew, and Coxswain Mr George Dyer, then aged 43, was awarded a bronze medal.

**FAIRWAY: 1-2 December 1978**

Naturally emergency calls come in the most anti-social hours and worst weathers. It was twenty to one in the morning when the coastguard alerted Captain Anderson to say that a 123 foot trawler called *Fairway* had engine trouble eight and a half miles south of Lyme Regis.

The *Fairway* had declined the services of a tug but had asked for a lifeboat to stand by. The Exmouth lifeboat was asked to launch but the Torbay one was prepared. When it turned out that low tide and heavy seas on the Exmouth bar prevented the Exmouth boat from going out, the Torbay boat was launched.

After establishing that the *Fairway's* engines could not be fixed, its skipper told the crew of six to put on their life-jackets and assemble midships for rescue.

The *Fairway* was rolling and pitching heavily in the rough seas, with waves measuring 30 feet from trough to crest. Then, making one run at a time to rescue one person at a time, the lifeboat began its task. This was to manoeuvre the lifeboat so as to prevent the two vessels from rolling together. The first person was rescued. On the second run alongside, four jumped together on to the lifeboat. Suddenly another man leapt on to the *Fairway's* trawl board but ended up hanging over the handrail with his legs and part of his body sticking overboard.

The Coxswain, Arthur Curnow, saw that large waves were coming up and that any minute the *Fairway* might roll towards the lifeboat and crush this man still hanging over the handrail. He put the engines to full astern, the lifeboat slipped out of danger and the man was rolled inboard, uninjured.

A headcount showed there was one man left on the *Fairway*. The lifeboat had to return alongside the rolling trawler and the sixth crewman promptly dived head first on to the foredeck of the lifeboat.

It was 7 a.m. when the task of the *Edward Bridges* was finally complete. Mr Arthur Curnow had only been elected to position of 1st Coxswain the previous month, and for his outstanding conduct in this and four other long services was specially commended.

Some night alerts are less hazardous. One spring evening the 'bleep' sounded at Captain Anderson's home. He phoned the Coxswain and then the lifeboat's volunteer crew were 'bleeped' in turn.

Five minutes later, the *Edward Bridges* ploughed out into the bay, crossing ribbons of silver moonlight shimmering on the calm water. As the lifeboat approached the drifting dinghy, which had been reported as possibly having someone on board, it focused a light on it.

A courting couple, heavily involved in a passionate embrace in the stern, looked up, startled and totally oblivious to the rest of the world. They received a tow back into harbour and no doubt the lifeboat crew amused their wives waiting their return at home when they told them the story.

*Bubble Trouble* is not the first daft name for a boat. This one was not so much a boat as a 'gin palace', an expensive 42-foot cruiser built 'purely for entertainment'.

'A flashing SOS light was reported to the coastguards by another ship,' said Captain Anderson, pointing out that this was unusual because a request for help is usually made by flares or radio.

'The lifeboat went out and found a big motor cruiser with two men on board who said they had run out of fuel. They said they were on their way from the Isle of Wight to Poole, in Dorset, but they were 70 miles westward and we never did find out why they had come so far this way.

'We towed them into Brixham and found these men were ferrying the boat to Poole for the owner. They had no charts, no lifesaving equipment or liferaft, no distress flares and no radio. But they had a fantastic galley, with a microwave oven and the latest kitchen gadgets, a bar with everything you can think of, and in the owner's cabin was a huge heart-shaped double-bed!'

Monsters of the sea off South Devon? Well, a little further out there are no monsters but friendly whales. And, like cows that scratch themselves on a solitary tree of a Devon field, whales evidently enjoy a good backscratch against the hull of a passing boat.

Passengers on a yacht out at sea beyond Torbay contacted the coastguard when they were surrounded by itchy whales and afraid they would capsize as one or two were scratching their backs on the bottom of the boat. The *Edward Bridges* was launched to rescue the novel scratching-post and Captain Anderson carefully filed this unusual mission for the RNLI's detailed records.

## BUTASEIS: 28 December 1979

The Torbay lifeboat's most hazardous mission was one which had the civic dignitaries of Brixham making contingency plans to prepare for a huge explosion.

The *Butaseis* was a Spanish coaster sheltering in Brixham harbour along with many other coasters during a south west force-

86

eight gale. Captain Anderson told the story:

'At eight o'clock in the morning they all eased away and started to sail. Suddenly a Spanish coaster, the *Butaseis,* called the coastguards and said: "I am on fire and abandoning ship." "Where are you?" it was asked. "Anchored off Brixham breakwater," came the reply.

'The coastguard looked out and saw the crew rowing like hell to shore and smoke coming from the back end of the coaster.

'Meanwhile, *Deneb,* a Dutch coaster, was going out and thought it would salvage the *Butaseis.* With the aid of the pilot cutter, it started towing it. We had by then launched the lifeboat. Then the Dutch crew thought to ask what cargo was on board the *Butaseis.* 740 tons of liquid butane gas! "We're going to make our tow rope as long as possible," they said.'

Everyone could see the huge gas bottles on the coaster and the police and fire brigade were alerted. London was informed, aircraft warned not to fly over the harbour, and a local committee headed by the Mayor was set up to consider the possibilities of an explosion and evacuating those nearest the harbour.

It turned out to be a long day, with the lifeboat crew putting out the fire that had begun in the *Butaseis* crew's cabin and also loaning a bucket to Royal Navy personnel whose rubber Zodiac dinghy filled with water and started to sink halfway across to the *Butaseis*!

With hindsight, it was clear that the gas bottles were unlikely to have blown up but for a time the lifeboat volunteers were prepared for a full-scale disaster.

Visitors and residents of South Devon are fortunate. They have a modern lifeboat and excellent communications between the coastguards, the lifeboat volunteers and local people who contribute in many ways to the service. All day and every day there are men supported by their wives ready to respond to any emergency off the South Devon coast.

The waves of the sea are mighty, it says in the Prayer Book. As long as there are people lured by the sea, there will be sea stories.

# THE KING OF BUCKS

*ROSEMARY ANNE LAUDER has been a regular contributor to* **The Bideford Gazette** *for several years, and lives just outside Bideford. This is her fourth contribution for Bossiney, her most recent being* **Exmoor in the Old Days,** *providing the text for 140 old photographs and picture postcards. She contributed to* **Strange Stories from Devon** *and wrote the text for* **Views of Old Devon.**

Just along the coast from Clovelly, built on the cliff overlooking the grey waters of Bideford Bay, is the tiny village of Bucks Mills. In the winter it is a dead, deserted place. Few of the cottages are occupied, the rest closed up, awaiting their rebirth with the annual influx of pleasure-bent holidaymakers in early summer.

Yet it was not always so. Within living memory every one of the dozen or so cottages was a home, with smoke rising from the chimneys, a well-scrubbed front doorstep, and cheerful lights shining a welcome from the windows. Sadly such villages are all too common in the Westcountry, but what makes Bucks Mills special is that once it was occupied almost entirely by one family—the Braunds.

Bucks and the Braunds were synonymous, and had been so ever since anyone could remember. Legends persisted that they were the descendants of shipwrecked Spaniards, possibly from the Armada, who came ashore at or near Bucks, married local girls, and took over the valley for their own. The Braunds, to this day, are strikingly different in looks from their Devonian neighbours, with glossy, dark hair and swarthy complexions, usually on the slim side and not over

◀ **Captain James Braund—'King of Bucks'.**

**Miss Olive Braund
and her father.**

tall—none of the comfortable 'Devonshire dumpling' look about the Braunds. They were a seafaring clan, risking death to wrest a poor living at fishing when the herring shoals off Clovelly were more plentiful than they are now.

Today there are only three Braunds still living at Bucks Mills. Olive Braund, who with Mr Len Braund of Bideford helped me compile this chapter, remembers the village in its heyday, when everyone was called Braund, and everyone was related. 'My grandfather had five brothers and four sisters, and apart from the eldest, who died young, they all had large families—eight or ten children maybe,' she recalls.

Her great grandfather was known as the 'King of Bucks' and to this day his cottage, perched on the very cliff edge, is known as King's Cottage. The King was one of those characters who appears somewhat larger than life. Captain James Braund was born in 1810, dying on 20 February 1898 at the venerable age of 88. His wife, Mary, had died four years previously aged 82, having borne him ten children.

James Braund became something of a legend in his own lifetime, no doubt his popular title of 'King' having been partly responsible.

90

He was by all accounts an expert sailor, born of a long line of sea-going folk, many of whom were master-mariners. He owned his own fishing boat and acted as pilot to coasting vessels. On several occasions he put to sea in hazardous conditions to save life and go to the aid of ships in distress. In 1873 a small pamphlet was published in his honour and underneath Captain James's picture was printed: 'Pilot over Bideford Bar for over forty years. Who Never Lost a Vessel or a Life.' Amongst the many instances of bravery recounted in this little book was the report given in the *Exeter and Plymouth Gazette* in 1850:

'On Monday, about half-past twelve o'clock at noon, a new American brigantine, belonging to Wm. Yeo, Esq., of Appledore, hove in sight in Bideford bay (being her first voyage from Prince Edward Island). She was observed by Captain James Braund, of Bucks, apparently in distress, and seeing a Clovelly boat approach her, but, whether from want of courage or practicability, return to the Pier, the undaunted heroism of the renowned fifth generation of Braunds sprung up; Capt. James and his brother launched a herring-boat through the surf, a tremendous sea running, followed the boat through the breakers, until they got her clear of the rocks, and succeeded in hoisting the reefed lug sail, made towards the brigantine; but the gale increasing, and the vessel driving towards the bar; the little Grace Darling was left to the mercy of a raging sea, and the Braunds had no alternative but to follow the vessel, then making the best of her way over the bar, as they found it impossible to return.

'The vessel, however, got into Appledore safe; meanwhile, the brave fellows in the boat had nothing but death before their eyes as a reward for their indefatigable exertions to render assistance to mariners in distress. Previous to taking the bar, they rigged the mizzen lug for a fore-sail, threw out half their ballast, and the mate pulled off his boots, expecting to have a swim for it, and when on the bar, the sea broke mountains high, behind and before them, but happily not on them; one sea set them right on end, and it was wonderful that the boat had not turned over with them.

'Numbers of people, looking at them on the hill at Appledore, exclaimed that it was impossible she could "live" to come through such a mad sea; yet, as nothing is impossible with Him who rules the storm, the brave fellows got into Appledore in safety, about three o'clock in the afternoon, after encountering the most miraculous enterprise of piloting on record. The good people of Appledore thronged around them on their arrival, heartily greeting them with expressions of gladness and praise for the skilful manner in which they managed their tiny prow, in the desperate situation in which they were placed. To describe the wailings and screams of the wives and children of the two Braunds is beyond power to express—they watched their progress as far up the bay as they could, with momentary expectation to see them "sink to rise no more".'

Newspaper reports of other brave deeds are included in the pamphlet, as well as a long poem in their praise beginning:

> *The Braunds of Bucks! The Braunds of Bucks!*
> *A race of hardy Men!*
> *So full of courage that their 'pluck'*
> *Eternally remain.*

A copy of the booklet was specially printed in Canada, and presented to all the descendants of Captain William Braund of Port Hope, Ontario. He was just one of the many Braunds who left the shores of North Devon for good, looking for a wider sea to sail. Another son, who qualified, as did so many of his ancestors and relatives, as a master mariner, made his home in New Zealand. Captain James Braund, born in Bideford in 1829, settled in Auckland where he married and had nine children, teaching all of them to sail in his topsail schooner.

Not surprisingly, today there are Braunds to be found all over the world, and in recent years a member of the family, Mr Cyril Braund of Bideford, has founded a Braund Society. It now has over 300 members, with its own history society and magazine. Closely involved with the genealogy and the history is Mr Len Braund, also of Bideford. He talks, as if he had known them all from childhood, of Braunds long dead who were characters of renown in the seventeenth, eighteenth and nineteenth centuries. 'The Braunds are a gifted race,' he said. 'Many of them became master-mariners before they were twenty-one. Others have risen to the top in all walks of life—in the church, in law, in commerce—and even in cricket with Leonard C. Braund, the Somerset County Cricketer, whose career spanned twenty-three years and included twenty-five centuries, and who was capped for England twenty-three times.'

Tales of many of them are recounted in the Braund Society magazine, including the story of the *Ebenezer*.

In the nineteenth century the glut of herrings was preserved for the winter by salting and storing in barrels. In many cases, salted herring was the only form of readily available food for the poorer families. However, salt was an unpopular cargo as it had to be kept dry. One winter there was a scarcity of this vital commodity and no Bideford skipper was prepared to make the long voyage to Spain for salt. So two of the Braunds, Richard and Reuben, decided to sail the *Ebenezer* to Lisbon and bring back as much salt as she could hold.

The *Ebenezer* was only a fishing smack and the Braunds set off at the worst time of year for such a voyage. Incredibly, only one week later reports reached Bucks Mills that the little boat had been sighted off Hartland Point. Later that day the sturdy vessel reached her home 'port' and unloaded her cargo on the beach where it was taken up to the village by cart. Reuben was the youngest son of Captain James, the 'King', who it is believed was himself the first skipper of the *Ebenezer*.

Visitors to Bucks Mills today may well wonder how it fostered so

**The King's cottage at Bucks Mills.**

**Two of the King's four sons.**

many redoubtable sailors. The beach is inhospitable—rocks and pebbles with no safe harbour or jetty to offer protection from the fierce gales that sweep across the bay, whipping the sea into a wild, tossing cauldron of waves and spume. A narrow channel, known as 'The Gore', between the beds of rocks, is Bucks Mills only claim to a refuge, and hard it must have been to make for this, the only fragile link with the shore and safety. Guiding lights still mark the channel, and solidly built limekilns and a sea-wall are testimony to generations of hardy men whose courage and seamanship brought renown to Bucks Mills.

What a remarkable family the Braunds must have been! It is said that strangers were not encouraged to visit Bucks and that any young man who dared to come courting one of the good-looking Braund girls would quickly be sent packing! Not surprisingly, inter-marriage was common, and Olive Braund's mother, a grand-daughter of the 'King', married another Braund, although not a close relative. She sadly remembers the times when the village hummed with life, when a Braund christening or wedding would set the whole community rejoicing, when she couldn't go outside her front door without meeting uncles, aunts, cousins, nephews. Now she lives on, in a cottage full of memories, and a street that echoes only to the past.

She gives the reasons for the departure of the Braunds, many of whom still live in neighbouring Clovelly and Bideford. They show no sign of dying out and Braunds are to be found scattered all over the globe, but sadly none have returned to live in the village that bred so many of them. Fishing and sailing had been a way of life to the Braunds for centuries, but by the end of the nineteenth century the world was a changing place. The herring shoals were decreasing, and the number of Braund children were increasing. Life at sea was hard and dangerous—one gravestone in the tiny churchyard at Bucks remembers Edward, drowned in sight of his home in 1897, aged twenty-nine years—and there must have been other Braunds who went to early, watery graves.

'The boys were all put to trades as soon as they were old enough,' Olive Braund told me. 'Then they all began to move away to be apprenticed. Their fathers had gone to sea in the summer, often sailing far from home on foreign ships, returning for the herring fishing in the winter.' The days of sail, however, were limited and large families needed a more stable livelihood. So gradually, over the years, the Braunds moved to wherever they could find work, and the cottages at Bucks reverted to their landlords, the Pine-Coffins of Portledge, and the great seafaring Braunds of Bucks became but a memory.

The colourful legend of the origin of the Braunds and their Spanish ancestors, refugees of the defeated Armada, taking the small fishing village by storm, have been disproved. The Braunds are believed to have originated at Braundsworthy in Black Torrington, with records going back possibly to the thirteenth century when the lord of the manor in the time of Henry II was a Sir Richard de Braundsworthy.

What brought them to the coast of North Devon is a mystery, but their striking looks and marked resemblance to each other is not disputed. The Braunds may well be the descendants of Iberian sailors who traded for Irish gold in the early Bronze Age and who may even have been shipwrecked off the North Devon coast. If so, their sea-going instincts remained strong and true down the countless generations of the Braunds of Bucks.

# PRINCE OF ROGUES
# LUNDY AND THOMAS BENSON

*DAVID YOUNG is one of the best known faces and voices in the Westcountry through his role as Television South West's roving architect. In 1983 he made his debut for Bossiney with* Around Glorious Devon. *A Yeovil resident, he is now working on* Somerset in the Old Days.

There can be no doubt in anyone's mind that we live on the most beautiful island in the world, which of course, explains our fascination for the tiny islands which surround our shores. For me, Lundy, twelve miles off the North Devon Coast, is the most enchanting of them all for it is virtually a miniature version of England: over the centuries it too has suffered traumas similar to those experienced on the mainland.

Lundy, about three miles long and half a mile wide, is basically a mass of granite, similar to that which forms Dartmoor, making it, in geological terms, at least fifty million years old. Protruding 400 feet or more from the sea at the entrance to the Bristol Channel, it has been occupied since prehistoric times; later by Vikings; by Royalist troops at the time of the Civil War and, of course, pirates during the eighteenth century.

Now owned by the National Trust, it was given to the nation by Mr Jack Hayward, and is administered by the Landmark Trust, who have restored the buildings, some interestingly enough as holiday accommodation.

◀ **Lundy Island's rugged coast.**

HMS *Montague* ran aground in thick fog in 1906 on
rocks at the south of Lundy.

Despite the presence of two lighthouses, the rugged coast has taken its toll of shipping over the years. Of the many vessels which have come to grief none can compare with HMS *Montagu*, which in 1906 in thick fog found itself on the rocks at the southernmost tip of the island. All four of her sister ships went to her rescue, but this show-piece of the Royal Navy, which had cost a million pounds to build, even in those days, proved impossible to refloat. Her crew of 750 men were taken off, without the loss of a single life. She was written off and now lies in about 50 fathoms below Shutter Rock.

A model of one of her sister ships is preserved on display in Millcombe House, now a hotel, situated at the head of the Millcombe Valley, on the sheltered eastern side of the island. The house was built by a former owner as a residence in 1836, in the Georgian style of architecture.

With an average population of twenty, buildings are few and far between on the island. Although Marisco Castle has undergone many alterations over the years it is still basically the fortress built 700 years ago. Above the Landing Beach are a small group of buildings bordering what is ambitiously called 'High Street'. They include the Marisco Tavern, a farm and surprisingly for so tiny a community, a massive parish church, which, built in 1896, can seat a congregation of sixty.

Ownership of the island has changed several times over the years and during the 1920s it belonged to the Harman family. In 1929 Martin Coles Harman decided to issue his own currency and 50,000 sets of 1 puffin and ½ puffin copper coins were minted. Understandably, in the circumstances, he included his profile on one side, whilst Lundy's most famous regular visitor, the puffin, filled the reverse side of the coin. The Royal Mint objected and he lost his case in the High Court. The coins today are collectors' items. Visitors can, however, still buy Lundy stamps, although if sending a card from the island put on an ordinary stamp as well, for they are not accepted by the Post Office.

Of all the people who have reigned over Lundy, none can compare with Thomas Benson for sheer bare faced effrontery. Few crooks in history can match his nerve and ingenuity. When you have heard his story I am sure you will agree that he deserves to be remembered as the king of con artists.

Although Benson became lessee of Lundy in 1748 it is important to go back a few years to trace this evil man's history. Having inherited the immense sum of £40,000, millionaire status by comparison in those days, he traded legally and quite successfully as a merchant in the busy North Devon port of Bideford. Because of his wealth he was held in great respect in the area and such was his influence within the community that he became Sheriff of Devonshire and ultimately entered Parliament in 1747, as member for the Barnstaple Division. This position of power was exactly what he had been seeking, for despite his wealth he sought to improve his fortune by criminal means.

The following year, 1748, the lease of the island was granted to him by the owner, Lord Gower, and it was then that Benson put his diabolical plan into operation. He contracted with the Government to ship convicts from Britain to the penal settlements in the Colonies; a quite legitimate, though unsavoury, trade in those days. What the authorities did not realise, however, was that the poor devils never made it to America—Benson shipped them instead to

**Approaching Landing Beach on Lundy. Marisco Castle stands on the headland.**

**St Helena's Church, Lundy—it can seat a
congregation of sixty!**

Lundy! Here they were set to work on Benson's behalf, quarrying
for granite, working on the farms and building the four walls which
today still quarter the island. What a scheme, for not only did he
make a huge profit by not taking them all the way to America, he
also had a continuous supply of slave labour to help build up his
empire.

Fiendish though such a scheme seems to us today it did not cause
Benson even one sleepless night. He is quoted as telling his closest
friends that '. . . the sending of the convicts to Lundy was the same
as sending them to America, they were transported from England,
it mattered not where it was as long as they were out of the
Kingdom.'

Although the authorities were unaware of his duplicity, one
doubts very much, had they known, whether they would have done
anything about it, had Benson not added yet another string to his
bow—that of smuggling.

Having successfully guarded his convict secret, even to the extent
of firing guns at passing ships to defend his kingdom, he then gave

**Lundy ponies.**

the game away by using the island as the headquarters of his smuggling operations. His exploits in that field were discovered and he was fined £5,000, a fortune in those days. Even then he would have got away with it if he had not defaulted on the fine. By refusing to pay what must have been for him a paltry sum, he became the architect of his own demise. The Sheriff of Devon went to the island to extract the fine and must have had the shock of a lifetime when he discovered Benson's kingdom of slaves.

The game was up and Benson fled to Portugal, his six year reign of terror over. The contraband was siezed, his estates on the mainland confiscated and one assumes, although there appears to be no record to the effect, that the luckless convicts continued their broken journey to the Colonies.

It would be nice to think that Thomas Benson received his just deserts and he might well have done so, but I have my suspicions that he continued his evil ways in Portugal for he did not die there until 1772. That such a man could survive a further eighteen years without resorting to his evil ways is doubtful. Certainly there is no evidence to support such a theory: but I wonder, perhaps unbeknown to us all, whether there is a tiny island off the Portuguese coast with an equally turbulent episode in its history—but one which didn't start until—1754!

# PLATE ACKNOWLEDGEMENTS

Front cover Naval History Library, Plymouth
Colouring by Paul Honeywill
Pages 5, 50 John Jeffery
Pages 6, 7 Royal Navy
Pages 8, 10, 11 Roy Westlake
Page 9 Alice Boyd
Page 12 Bossiney Library
Page 13 David C. Golby
Pages 16, 70 Paul Honeywill
Page 19 Plymouth City Museum
Page 23 H. & B. Graeme, Noah's Ark
Pages 27-31, outside back cover Nicholas Toyne
Pages 35-47 Britannia Royal Naval College, Dartmouth
Pages 48-57 Captain P.M. Herbert
Page 53 George Ellis
Pages 59-66 The Royal Navy Submarine Museum, Gosport
Page 72 Local History Library, Plymouth
Page 69 Felicity Young
Pages 75, 77 Ray Bishop
Page 79 upper Herald Express
Page 79 lower Chris Bryan, Torbay News
Pages 80-83 David Williams, Herald Express
Page 88 Bucks Parochial Hall
Pages 90, 94 by courtesy of Miss O. Braund
Page 93 Sandra Yeo
Pages 96, 100-102 Joan Rendell
Page 98 Waverley Photographic Ltd

# ALSO AVAILABLE

## STRANGE STORIES FROM DEVON
by Rosemary Anne Launder and Michael Williams.
46 photographs.
Strange shapes and places—strange characters—the man they couldn't hang, and a Salcombe mystery, the Lynmouth disaster and a mysterious house are only some of the strange stories.
'*A riveting read.*'                                                  The Plymouth Times
'*. . . well-written and carefully edited.*'
                                   Monica Wyatt, Teignmouth Post & Gazette

## AROUND GLORIOUS DEVON
by David Young. 148 photographs.
David Young, well known in the Westcountry as TSW's roving architect, takes us on a personally-conducted tour of his glorious Devon.
'*. . . proves as good a guide in print as he is on the small screen.*'
                                             Judy Diss, Herald Express

## VIEWS OF OLD PLYMOUTH
by Sarah Foot.
Words and old pictures combine to recall Plymouth as it once was: a reminder of those great times past and of the spirit of the people of Plymouth.
'*This is a lovely nostalgia-ridden book and one which no real Plymothian will want to be without.*'
                                   James Mildren, The Western Morning News

## VIEWS OF OLD DEVON
Rosemary Anne Lauder provides the text for more than 200 postcards, evocative of a world and a way of life that has gone.
'*Only the camera can turn back the clock like this.*'          The Sunday Independent

## MY DEVON
Ten writers writing about their Devon: Hugh Caradon, Judy Chard, Andrew Cooper, Robin Davidson, Daniel Farson, Sarah Foot, Clive Gunnell, James Mildren, Mary and Hal Price.
'*. . . ten writers' impressions of their favourite places . . . the personal approach warms and enlivens . . .*'
                                                            Herald Express

## GHOSTS OF DEVON
by Peter Underwood. 44 photographs and drawings.
Peter Underwood, President of the Ghost Club, writes of the ghostly stories that saturate the County of Devon, a land full of mystery and of ghostly lore and legend.
'*Packed with photographs, this is a fascinating book.*'          Herald Express